# THE OLD LANDMARK

Featuring a Collection of Songs from Southern Gospel's Finest

Arranged and Orchestrated by Wayne Haun

lillenas.com

# Contents

# The Old Landmark

Words and Music
Traditional
*Arr. by Wayne Haun*

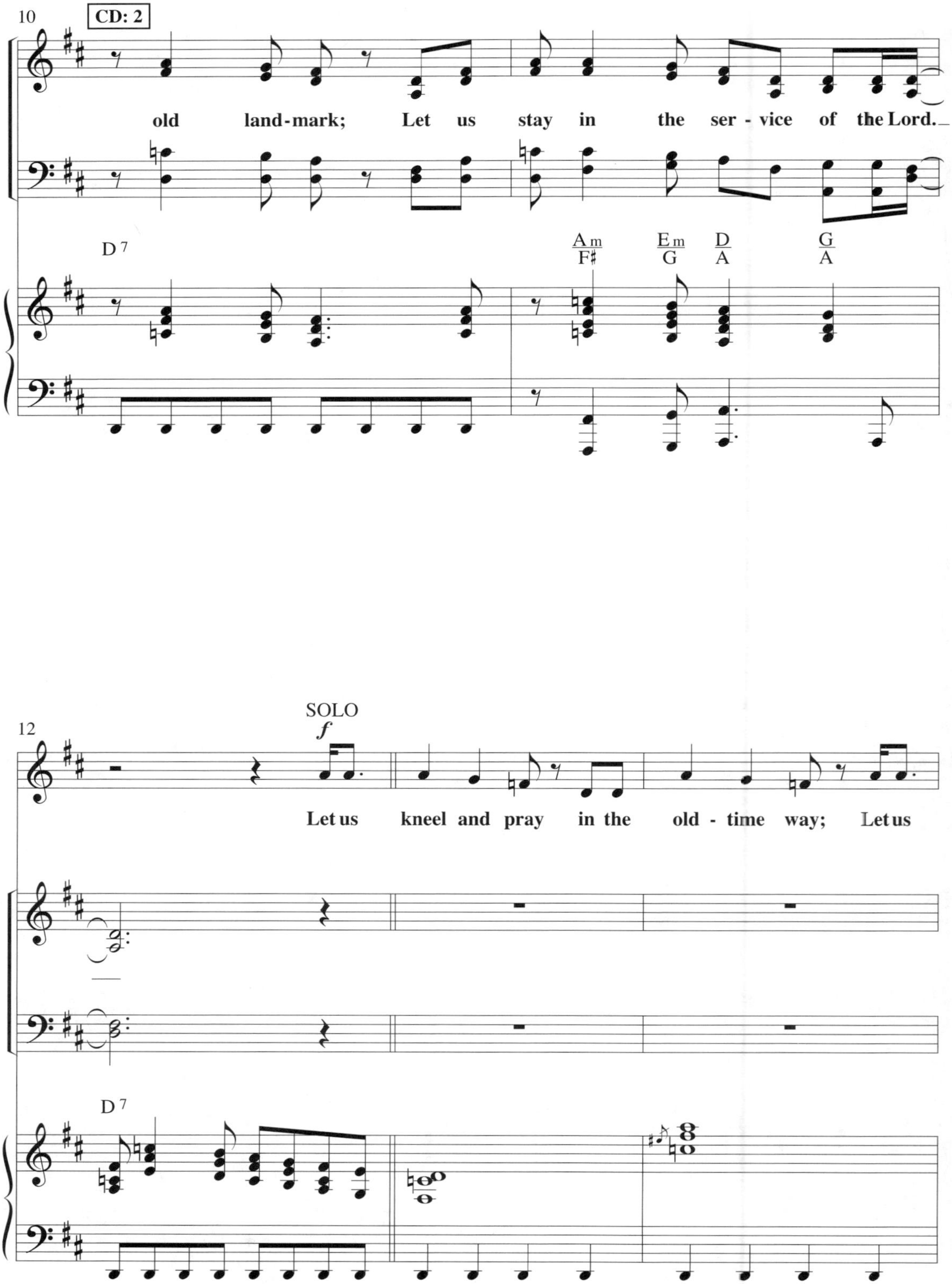

12

SOLO

*f*

Let us kneel and pray in the old - time way; Let us

D 7

15
kneel and pray in the old - time way; Let us
G 7
D 7
17
kneel and pray in the old - time way; He will
D 7
19
and be We'll be bread from Tell the
f
Hear us, near us; Giv - en, heav - en;
f
D 7

21

CD: 3

of His It will it will It will

Sto - ry, glo - ry; Warn them, turn them;

D7

23

save this old world from sin and shame. Well, I wan - na see a

Save this old world from sin and shame.

Am/F♯ Em/G D/A G/A D7 B♭7

25
big re - viv - al in the old - time way;
E♭7
27
I wan-na see a big re-viv - al in the old - time way; I wan - na see a
A♭7
E♭7
29
big re-viv - al in the old - time way;
Sin - ners,
E♭7

31

learn - ing, turn - ing, yearn - ing; burn - ing; hear

con - verts; Chris - tians, fi - re; He will,

E♭7

33

CD: 4

us near us; warn them, It will turn them;

and be; It will, it will; It will

E♭7

35
Come on
save this old world from sin and shame.
B♭m/G
Fm/A♭
E♭/B♭
A♭/B♭
E♭7
B
37
down to the riv-er in the old-time way; Come on
E7
39
down to the riv-er in the old-time way; Well,
A7
E7

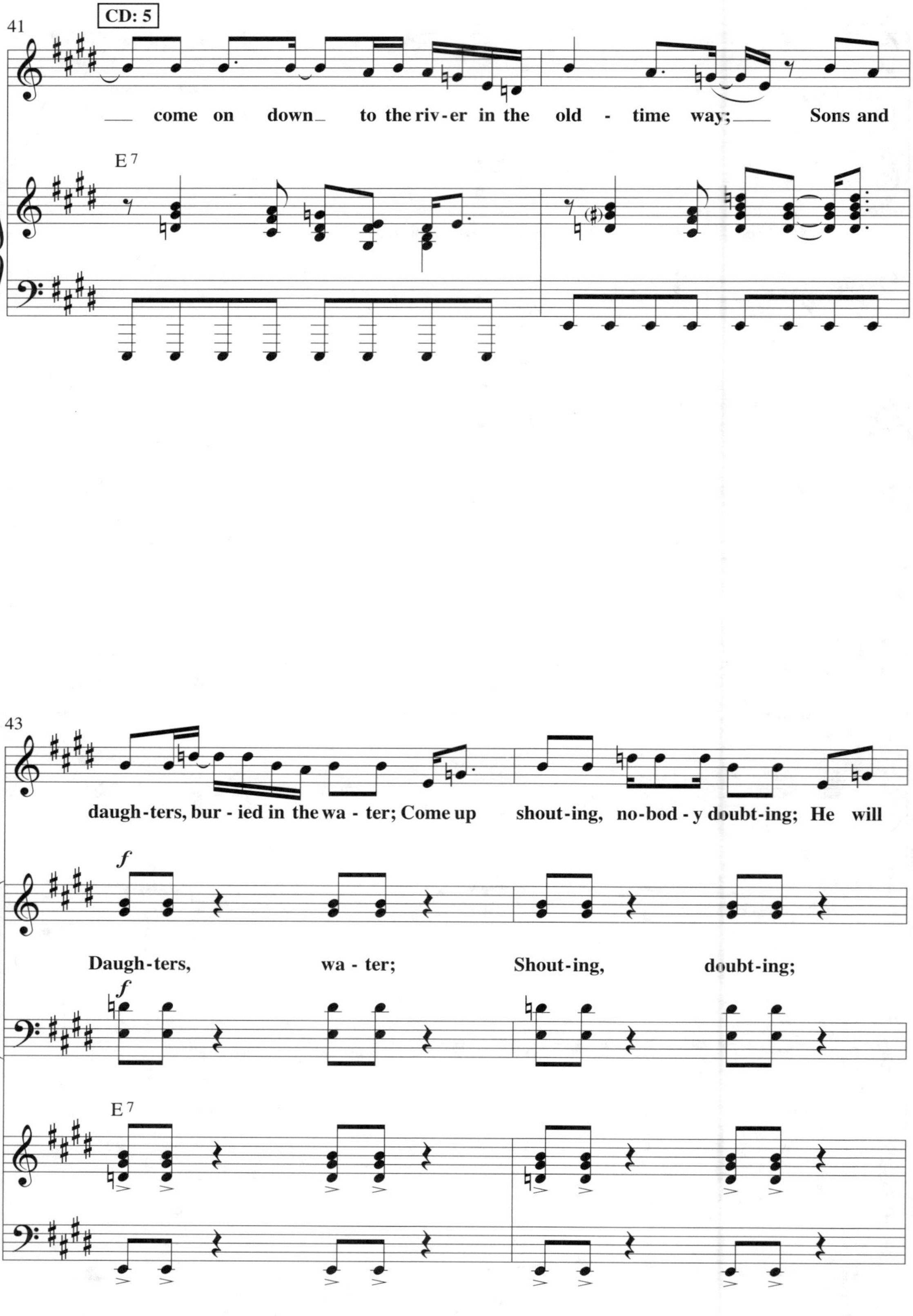

43

daugh-ters, bur - ied in the wa - ter; Come up shout-ing, no-bod - y doubt-ing; He will

*f*

Daugh-ters, wa - ter; Shout-ing, doubt-ing;

*f*

E 7

45

hear us, and be near us; We'll be giv - en bread from heav - en; Tell the

Hear us, near us; Giv - en, heav - en;

E7

47

sto - ry of His glo - ry; It will warn them, it will turn them; Ev-'ry-bod-y

Sto - ry, glo - ry; Warn them, turn them;

E7

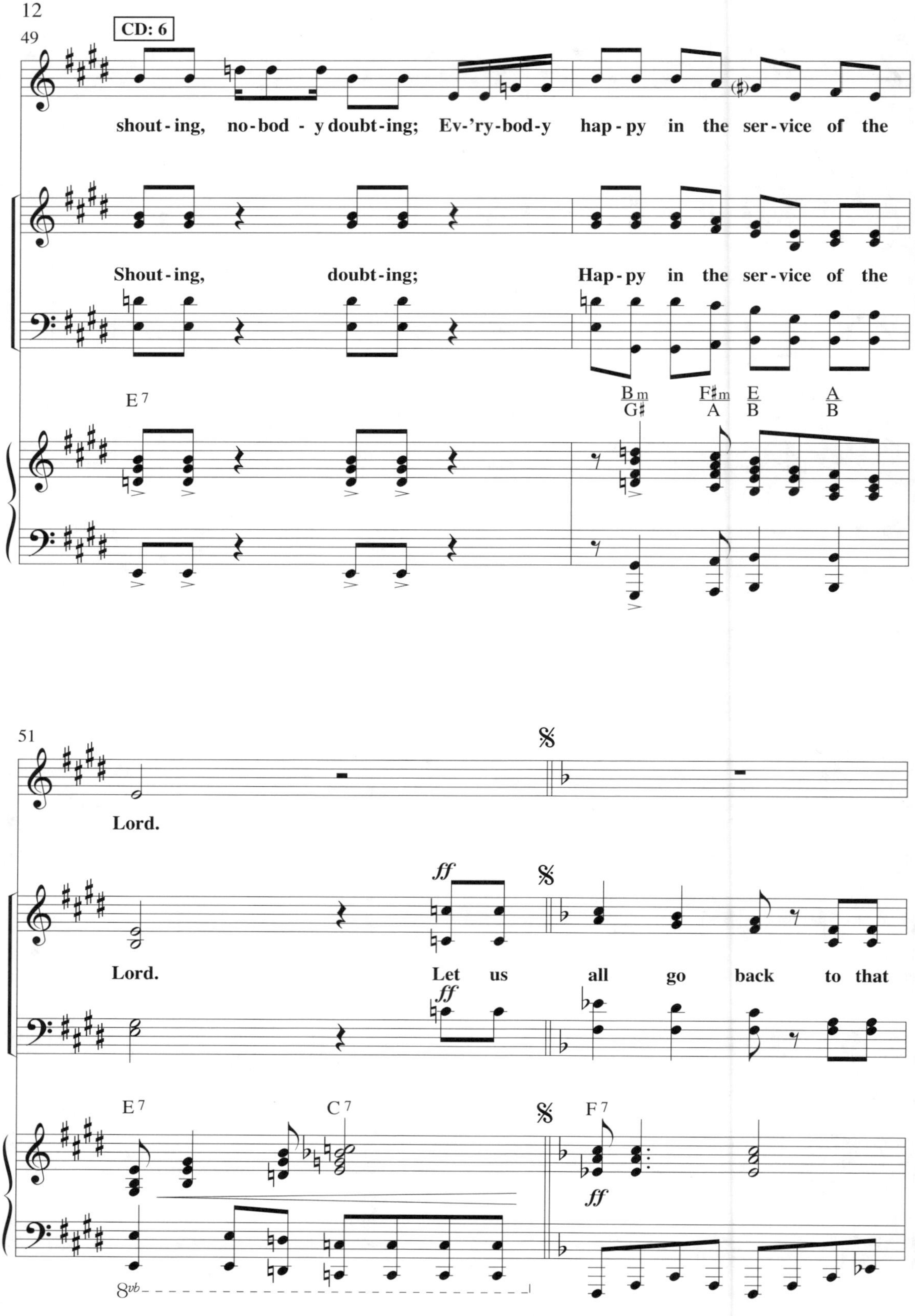
CD: 6
49
shout - ing, no-bod - y doubt - ing; Ev-'ry-bod-y hap - py in the ser - vice of the
Shout - ing, doubt - ing; Hap - py in the ser - vice of the
E7
Bm/G♯ F♯m/A E/B A/B
51
Lord.
Lord.
ff
Let us all go back to that
ff
E7 C7
F7
ff
8vb

53
old land-mark; Let us all go back to that
F7
B♭7
55
old land-mark; Now let us all go back to that
F7
57
old land-mark; Let us stay in the ser-vice of the Lord.
F7
Cm/A
Gm/B♭
F/C
B♭/C

59
F 7
OPTIONAL REPRISE
62
Fine
CD: 7
OPTIONAL REPRISE
F 7
Fine
F 7
f
65
D.S. al Fine
(to pg. 12, meas. 52)
ff
Let us
ff
F 7
cresc.
D.S. al Fine
(to pg. 12, meas. 52)

# Heaven Will Be My Reward

*with*

Heaven Will Surely Be Worth It All

Words and Music by
WAYNE HAUN and
LILLIE KNAULS
*Arr. by Wayne Haun*

With conviction, light swing ♩ = ca. 113 (♫ = ♩ ♪)

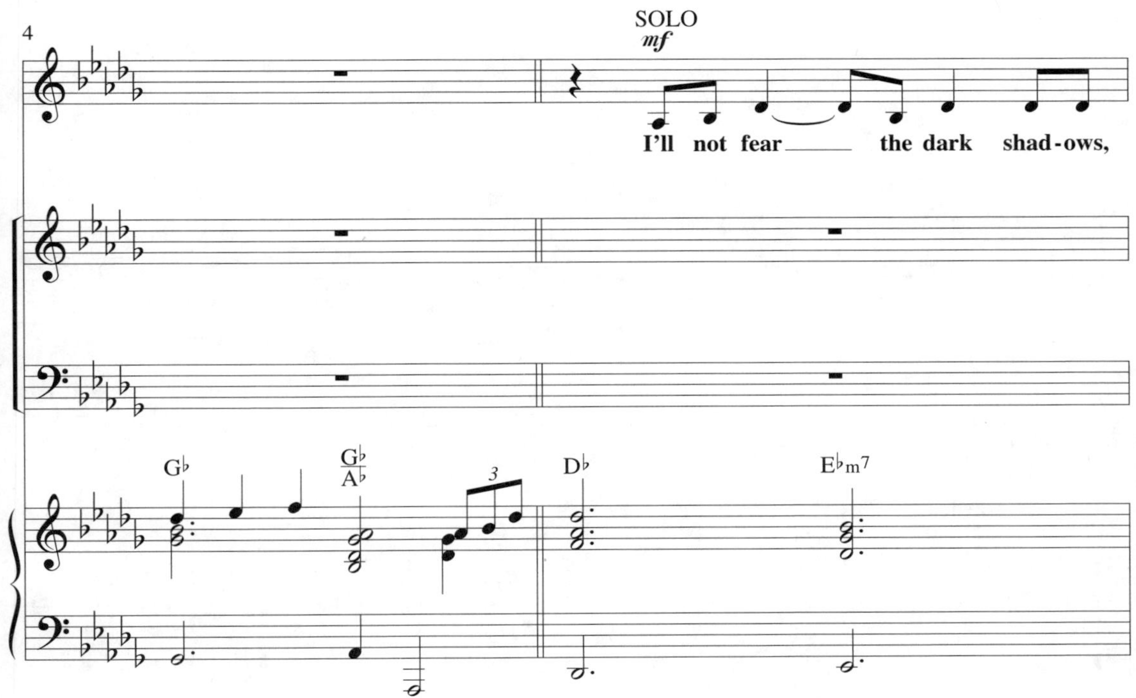

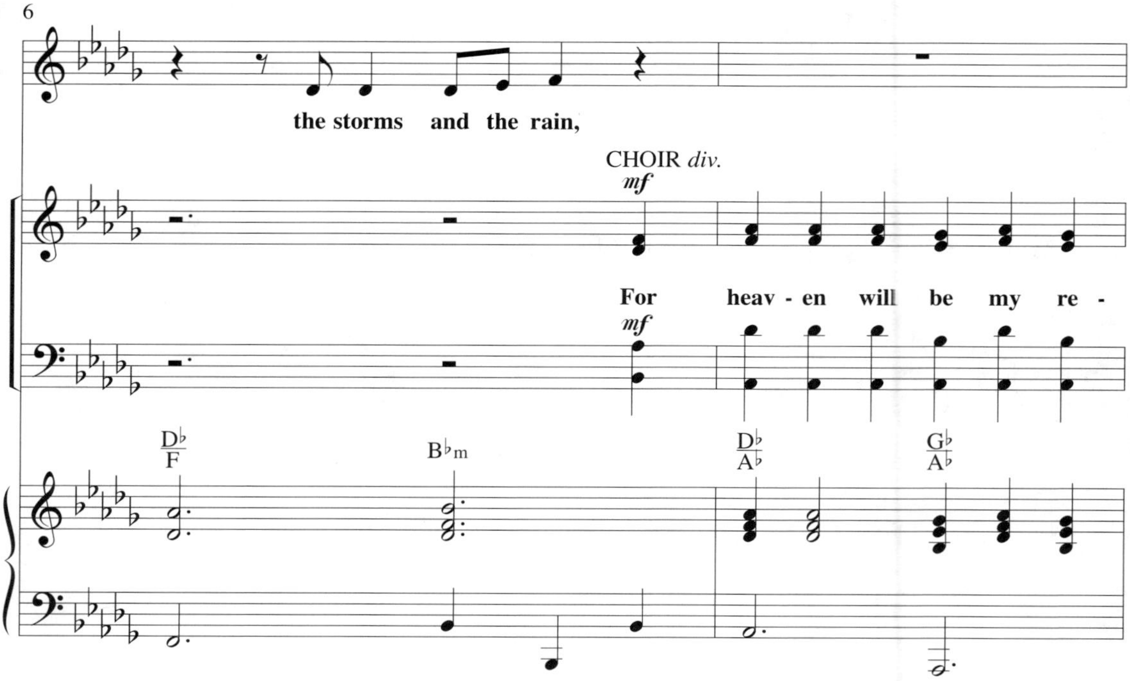

6

the storms and the rain,

CHOIR *div.*

*mf*

For heav - en will be my re -

*mf*

D♭/F B♭m D♭/A♭ G♭/A♭

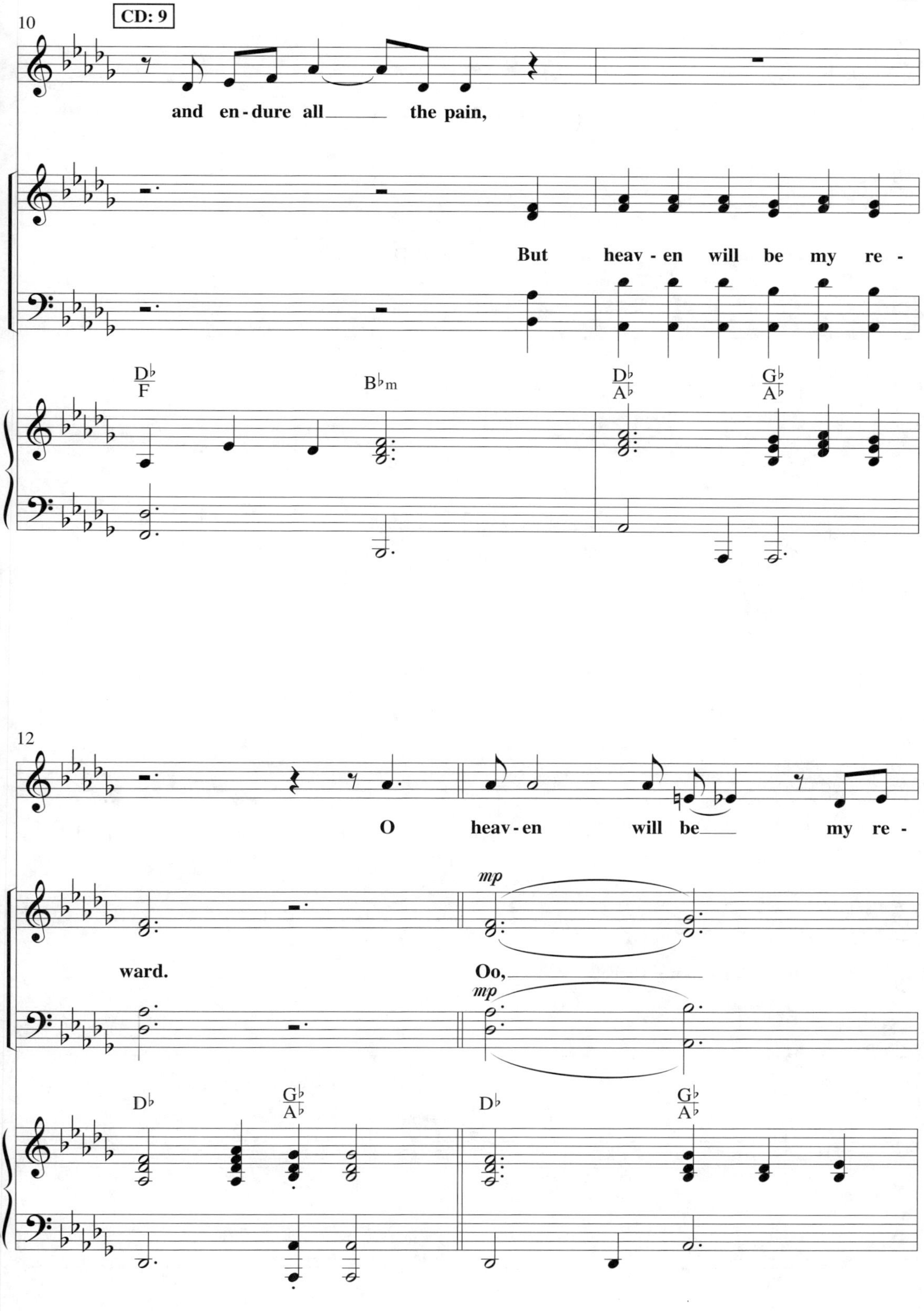

10

CD: 9

and en - dure all ___ the pain,

But heav - en will be my re -

D♭/F B♭m D♭/A♭ G♭/A♭

14

ward, When I cross o - ver to Jor - dan's

be my re - ward, Oo,

D♭ D♭/F G♭

16

shore; I will lay down my crown at the

to Jor - dan's shore; Oo,

D♭ B♭m A♭/C

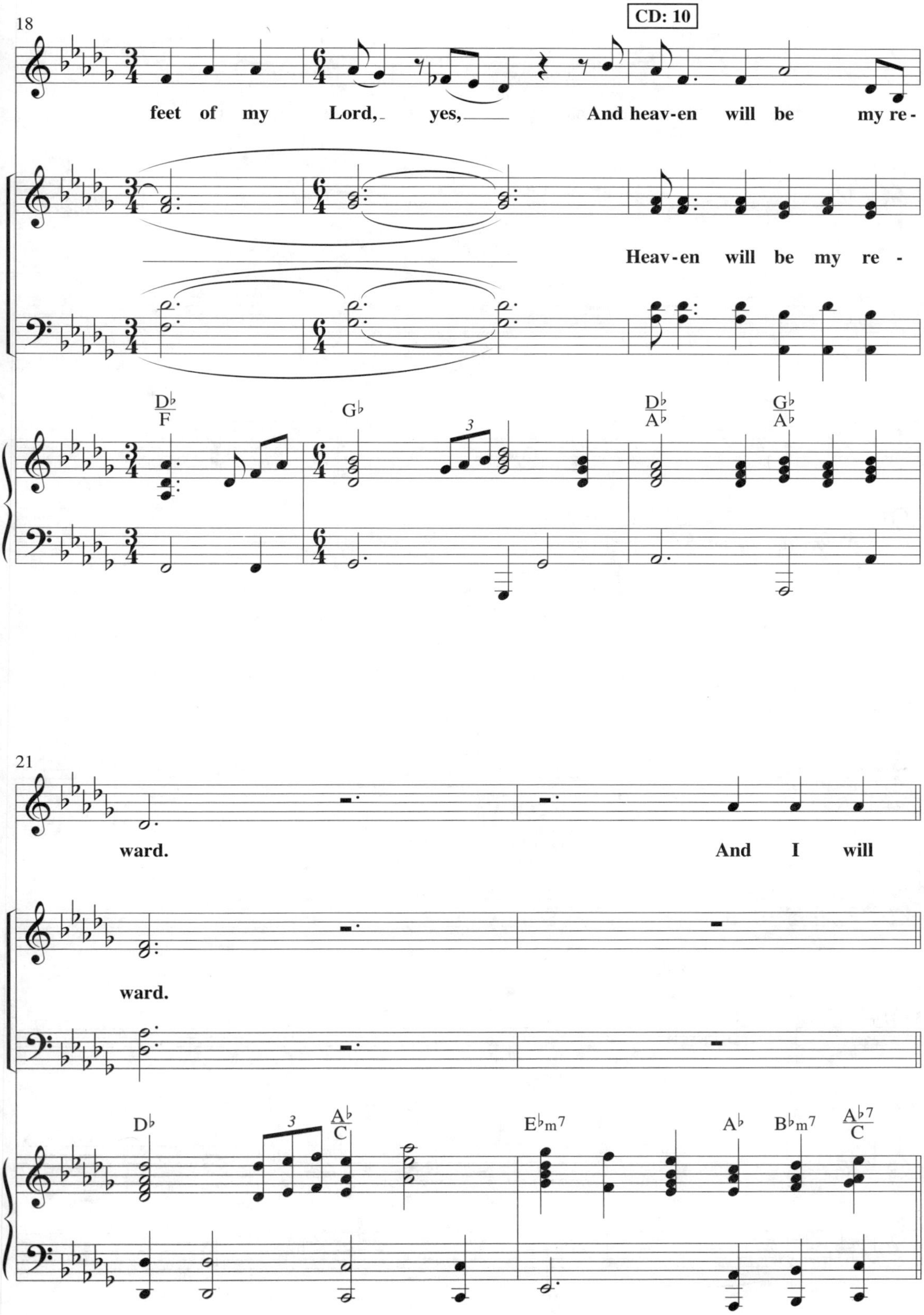

18

CD: 10

feet of my Lord, yes, And heav-en will be my re-

Heav-en will be my re-

D♭/F G♭ D♭/A♭ G♭/A♭

23

press toward the goal as this race I run,

*mf*

And

*mf*

D♭ E♭m7 D♭/F B♭m

25

O the

heav - en will be my re - ward;

D♭/A♭ G♭/A♭ D♭ G♭/A♭

27

CD: 11

cresc. f

joy that is wait-ing when He says, "Well done," And

mp f

Oo, "Well done."

mp f

D♭ E♭m7 D♭/F B♭m

29

heav - en will be my re - ward. I'm so glad,

Heav-en will be my re - ward.

D♭/A♭ G♭/A♭ D♭ G♭/A♭

f

31

heav - en will be my re - ward, O when I

Heav - en will be, be my re - ward,

D♭ G♭/A♭ D♭ D♭/F

33

cross o - ver to Jor - dan's shore; I will

Oo, to Jor - dan's shore;

G♭ D♭

35

lay down my crown at the feet of my Lord, O and

*mf*

Oo, my Lord, And

*mf* *f*

B♭m A♭/C D♭/F G♭

38 CD: 12

heav-en will be my re-ward, yes.

heav-en will be my re - ward.

D♭/A♭ G♭/A♭ D♭ G♭/A♭

*"Heaven Will Surely Be Worth It All"

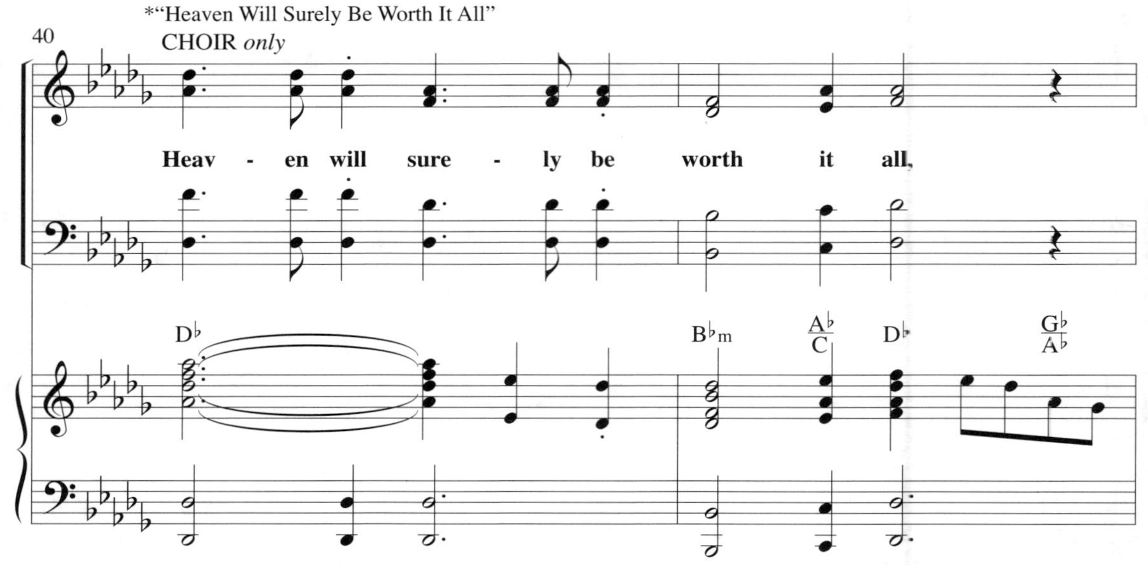


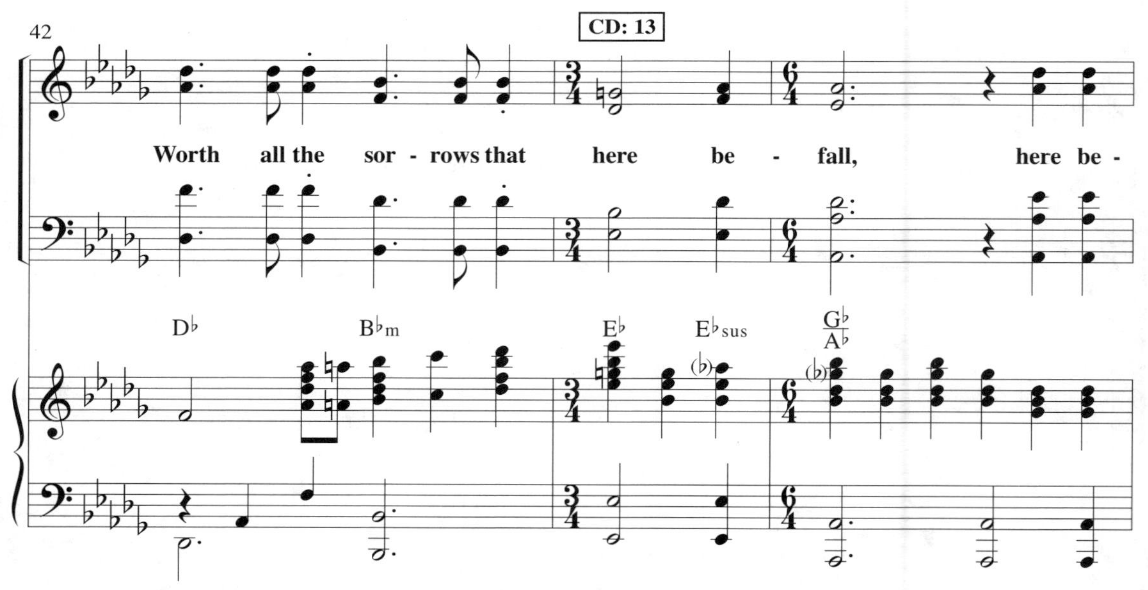

45
SOLO
We're gon-na lay down all our crowns
fall. Oo,
G/A A A♯°7 Bm A/C♯
47
at the feet of our lord, of the Lord; And
our Lord, feet of our lord,
D/F♯ G D/F♯ G

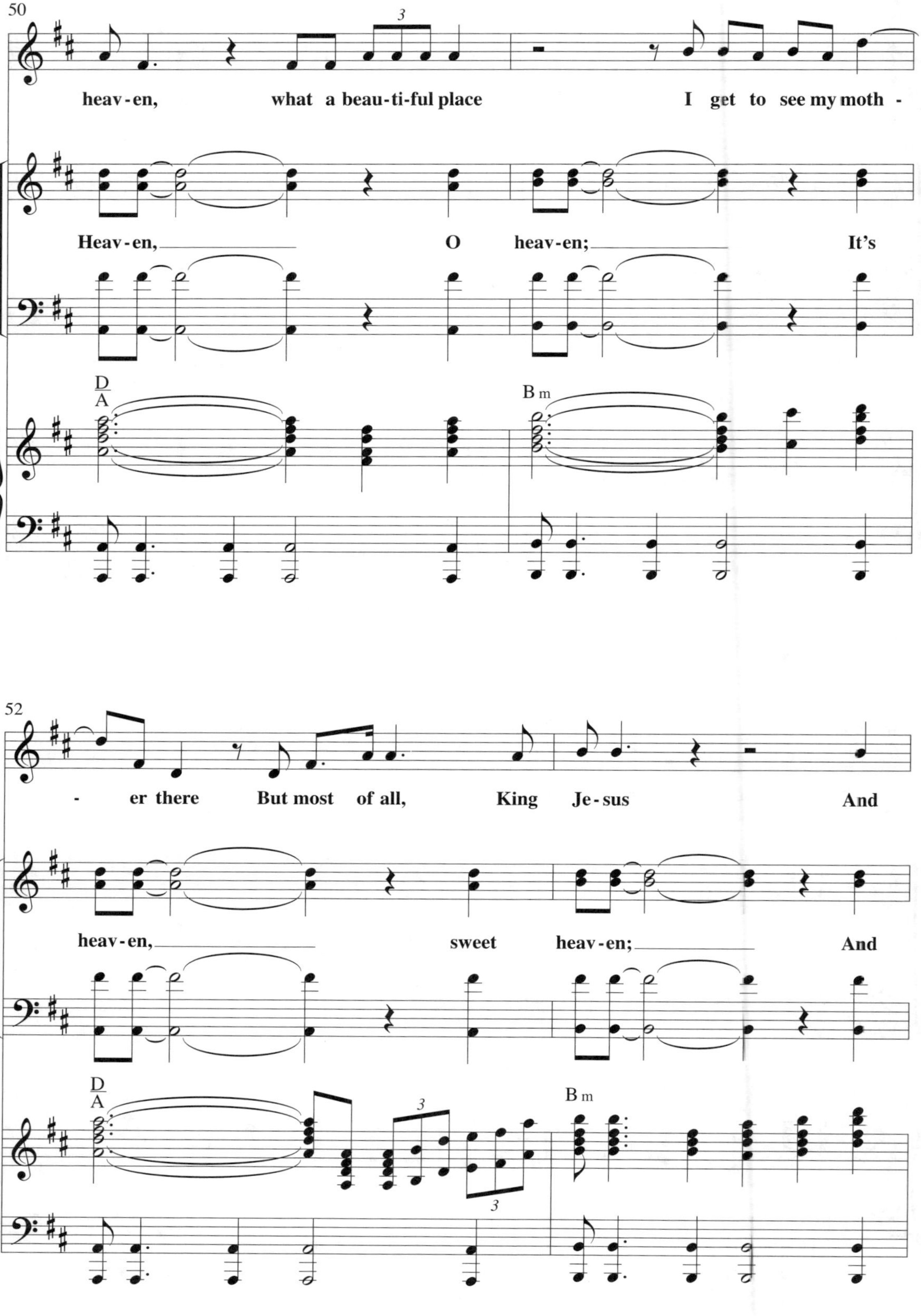

50

heav - en, what a beau - ti - ful place I get to see my moth -

Heav - en, O heav - en; It's

D/A

Bm

52

- er there But most of all, King Je - sus And

heav - en, sweet heav - en; And

D/A

Bm

54

heav-en will be my re-ward,

heav-en will be my re - ward,

D/A A7 D

56

be my re - ward. O yeah.

be my re - ward.

D

8vb

# He Found Me

Words and Music by
WAYNE HAUN, JOEL LINDSEY
and JASON CLARK
*Arr. by Wayne Haun*

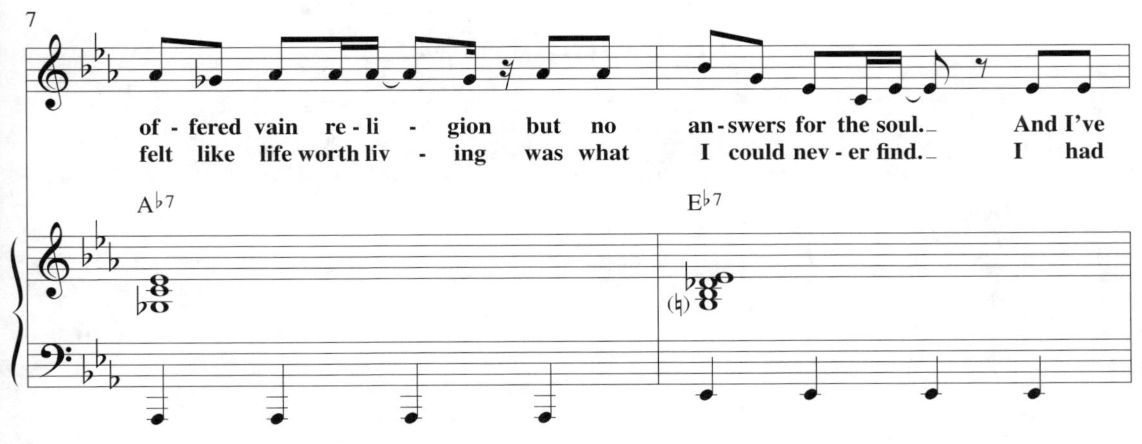
7
of - fered vain re - li - gion but no an - swers for the soul. And I've
felt like life worth liv - ing was what I could nev - er find. I had
A♭7
E♭7

9
read the an - cient writ-ings of the world's phi - los - o - phies; And I
searched the whole world o - ver for sal - va - tion I could feel; And with
E♭7

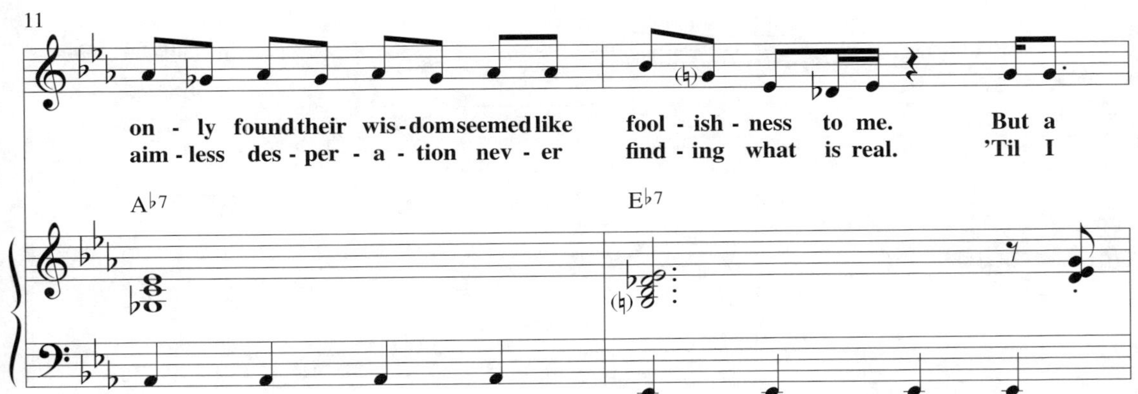
11
on - ly found their wis - dom seemed like fool - ish - ness to me. But a
aim - less des - per - a - tion nev - er find - ing what is real. 'Til I
A♭7
E♭7

CD: 15 *1st time*

CD: 17 *2nd time*

13

dust - y worn out Bi - ble that I've cher - ished since my youth; Is
turned my eyes to Je - sus thro' the pag - es of His word; And

CHOIR *div.*

**mf**

Oo,

**mf**

G7sus G7 Cm

15

SOLO *joins Choir*

where I found the on - ly thing that gave me hope and truth.
there I found such joy and peace in what I'd seen and heard.

**f**

Oo.

'Cause I found

**f**

G7sus G7 Cm A♭/B♭ A♭7♭5

17
Je - sus in the pag - es of that bless - ed book; And I
A♭7
19
found Him in the man - ger where the an - gel said to look.
I
E♭7
21
found Him at the tem - ple teach - ing schol - ars of His day;
I
A♭7

23

SOLO

*f*

Then I

found Him with the crip-pled with the blind and with the lame.

F7 B♭7

25

found Him walk - ing wa - ter on the sea of Gal - i-lee; And I

*mf*

Oo,

*mf*

And I

E♭ D♭/E♭ E♭ D♭/E♭ E♭7

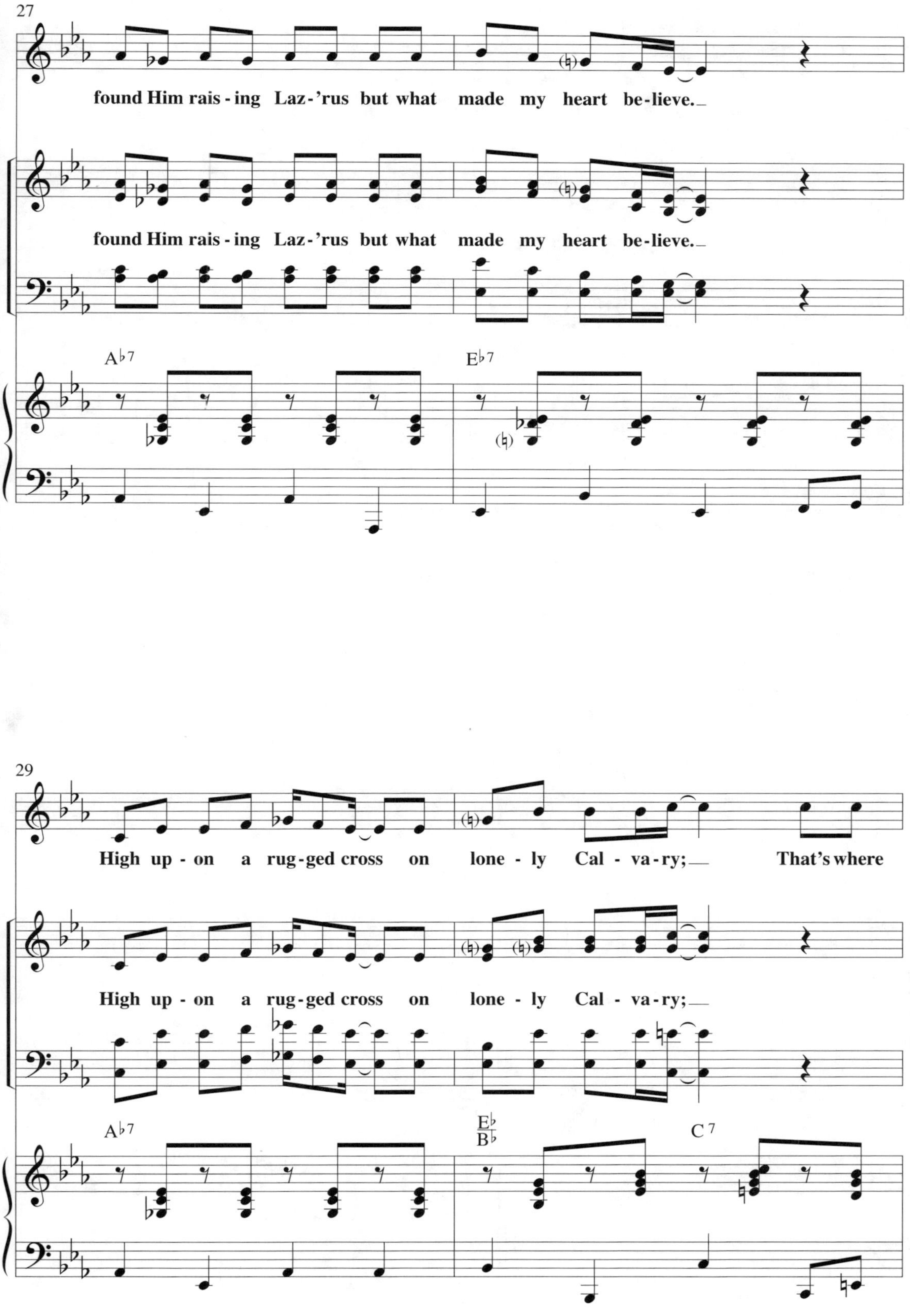

27

found Him rais - ing Laz - 'rus but what made my heart be - lieve.

found Him rais - ing Laz - 'rus but what made my heart be - lieve.

A♭7

E♭7

CD: 16 *1st time*
CD: 18 *2nd time*

31

1

Je - sus, where He found me.

Where He found me.

F7 A♭/B♭ 1 E♭7

33

(to pg. 28, meas. 5) 2

SOLO *f*

2. I had me.

me.

(to pg. 28, meas. 5) 2

E♭7 E♭7

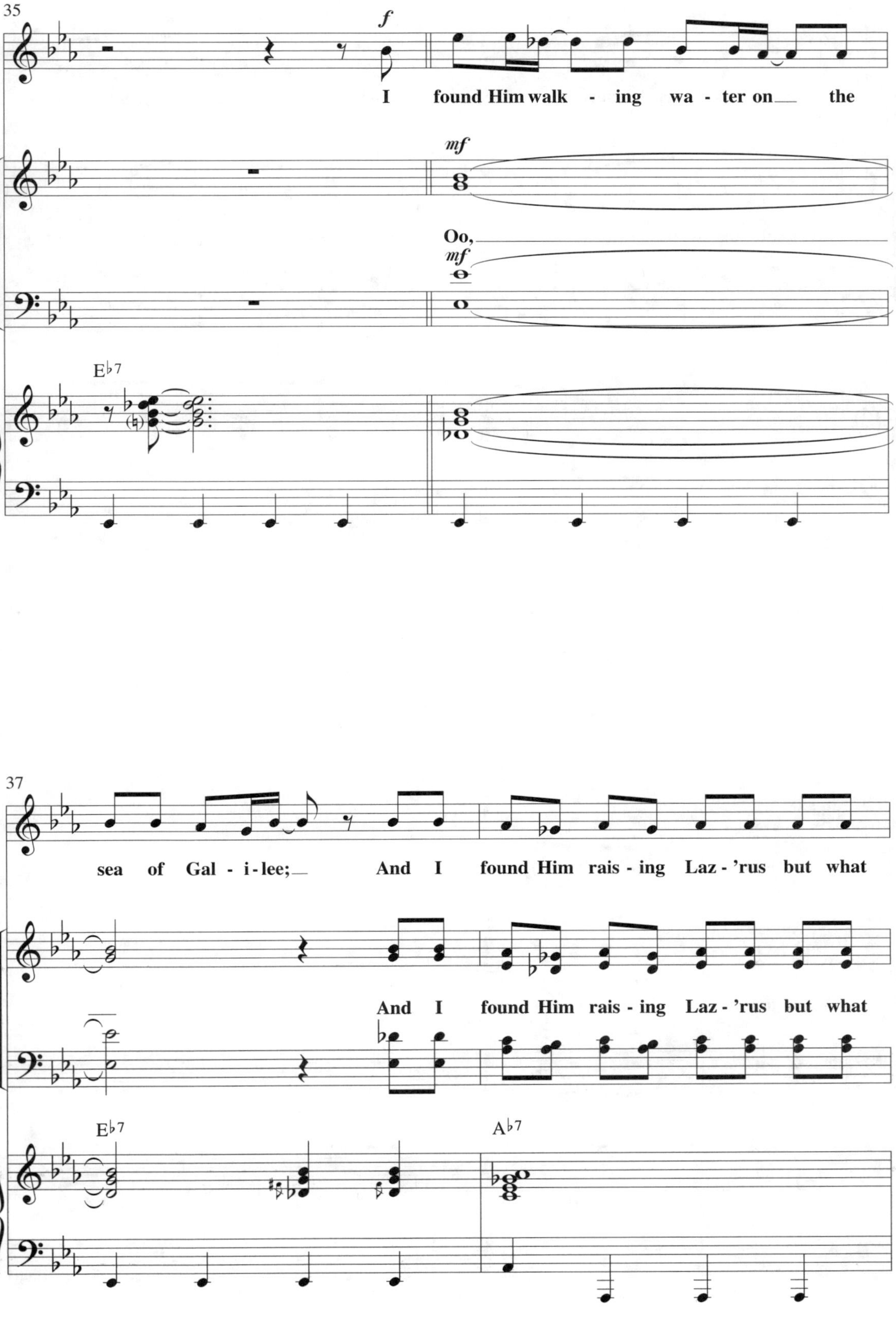

35

*f*

I found Him walk - ing wa - ter on the

*mf*

Oo,

*mf*

E♭7

39

made my heart be-lieve._ High up - on a rug-ged cross_ on

made my heart be-lieve._ High up - on a rug-ged cross_ on

*f*

E♭7 A♭7

41

CD: 19

lone - ly Cal - va - ry;_____

lone - ly Cal - va - ry;_____

E♭/B♭ C7

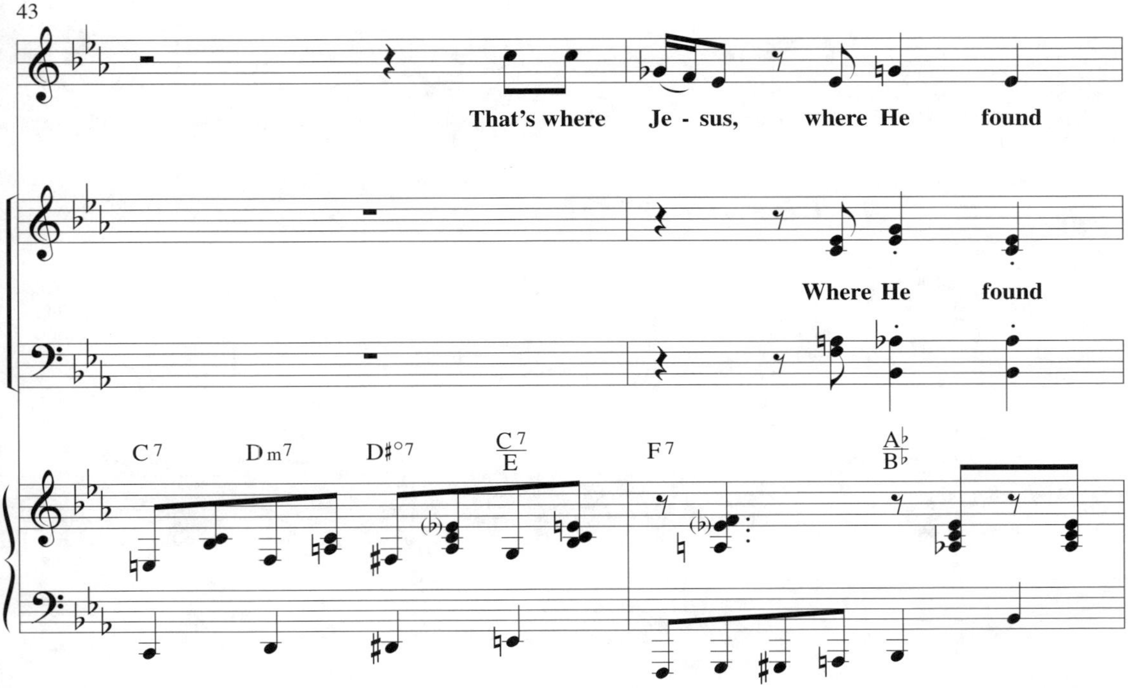
43
That's where Je - sus, where He found
Where He found
C7 Dm7 D♯°7 C7/E
F7 A♭/B♭

45
me, He found me. That's where Je - sus, where He found
me. Where He found
E♭ C7
F7 A♭/B♭

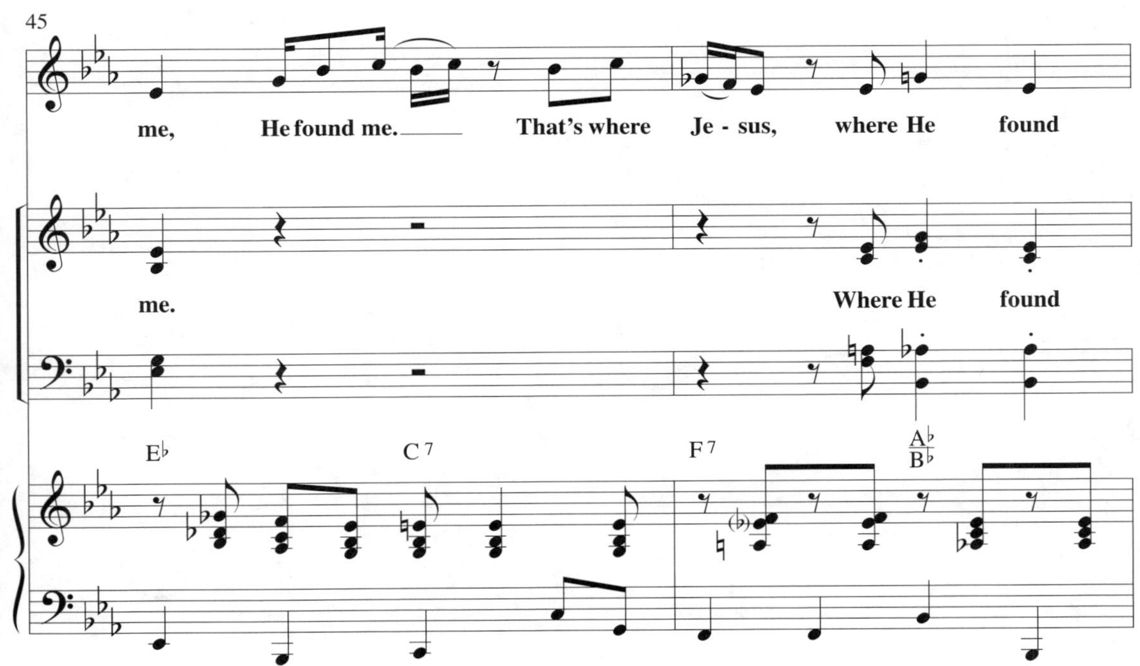

47

me, He found me. That's where Jesus, where He found

me. Where He found

E♭ C7 F7 A♭/B♭

49

me.

me.

E♭7 D♭/E♭ A♭/E♭ E♭7

8vb

# Oh the Thought That Jesus Loves Me

Words and Music by
WAYNE HAUN
and LYN ROWELL
*Arr. by Wayne Haun*

10
More than I can un - der-
G♭
D♭
D♭7
13
stand;
Fills my heart
G♭
D♭7sus
G♭
16
with calm as - sur - ance,
I am
G♭

CD: 21
19
safe
in - side His plan.
D♭
D♭7
G♭
22
f
I will let
it change and
f
G♭
G♭7sus
A♭
G♭7
B♭
C♭
f
25
heal me,
Let it ease
G♭

28
mf
my trou - bled mind;
Oh, the
G♭
E
D♭
E♭m7
D♭7/F
31
thought
that Je - sus loves me,
G♭
G♭7/B♭
C♭
G♭
mf
34
CD: 22
That He loves
me for all
G♭
E♭m7
D♭sus
D♭
D♭7sus/E♭
D♭7/F

37
mf
time.
Oh, the thought
mf
G♭
G♭/D♭
D♭7sus
G♭
mf
40
that Je - sus loves me,
Loved when
G♭
43
we were far a - part;
D♭
D♭7
G♭

46
When my will was set a -
G♭
D♭7sus
G♭
49
gainst Him, Loved e - nough
G♭
D♭
52
CD: 23
to win my heart.
D♭7
G♭
C♭2

55 SOLO *mf*

Oh, the thought that Je - sus

G C2 G

59

loves me, That He'd choose

G D

62

a cross to die; Take the

D7 G D7sus

65

death I was de - serv - ing,

G

CD: 24

68

— Just to — of - fer me — new life.

G D D7 G

78
my trou - bled mind;
Oh, the
G
F
D
Em7
D7/F♯
81
thought
that Je - sus loves me,
G
G7/B
C
G
84
That He loves
me for all
G
Em7
Dsus
D
D7sus/E
D7/F♯

87
mp
time.
Oh, the thought
mp
G
mp

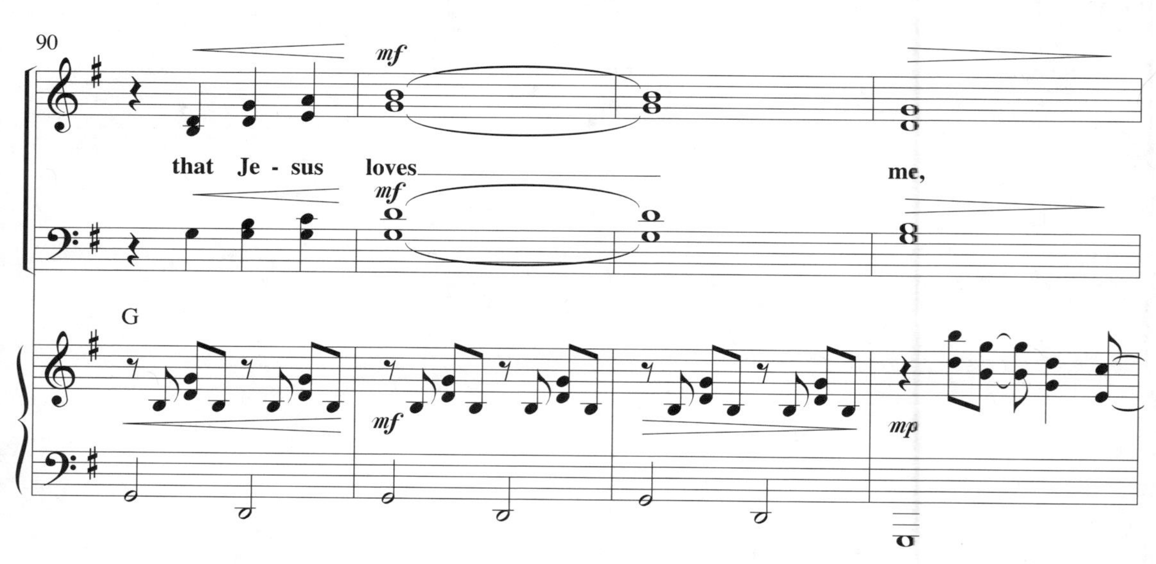
90
mf
that Je - sus loves
me,
mf
G
mf
mp

C2
C
D
G
C2
G 4 2
C
G
94
rit.

# The Blood of Jesus

*with*

The Blood Will Never Lose Its Power

7

cleanse your deep-est sin. *mf* The blood of Je-sus, the

A/E E A D/F♯ E/G♯ A Bm/A A

*mf*

10

*f*

blood of Je-sus, The blood of Je-sus, can

A Bm/A A Em/C♯ D D/A A A/C♯ D

*f*

12

**CD: 26**

cleanse your deep-est sin.

A/E E A D/A

*dim.*

14
SOLO
mf
You may think you've gone too far,
You may think there is no pow'r;
A
E
Em
C♯
D

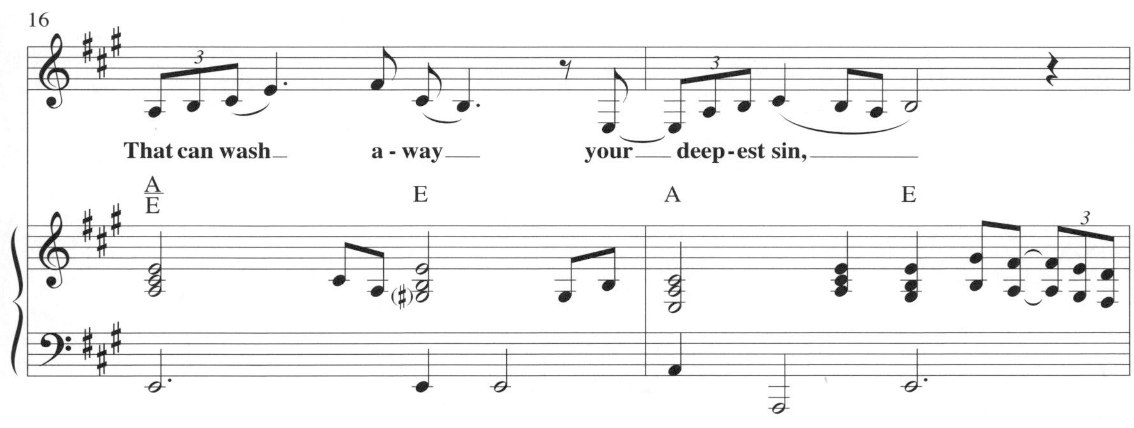
16
That can wash a - way your deep-est sin,
A
E
E
A
E

18
There is hope for you, my friend;
Je - sus died and rose a - gain, So that
A
E
Em
C♯
D

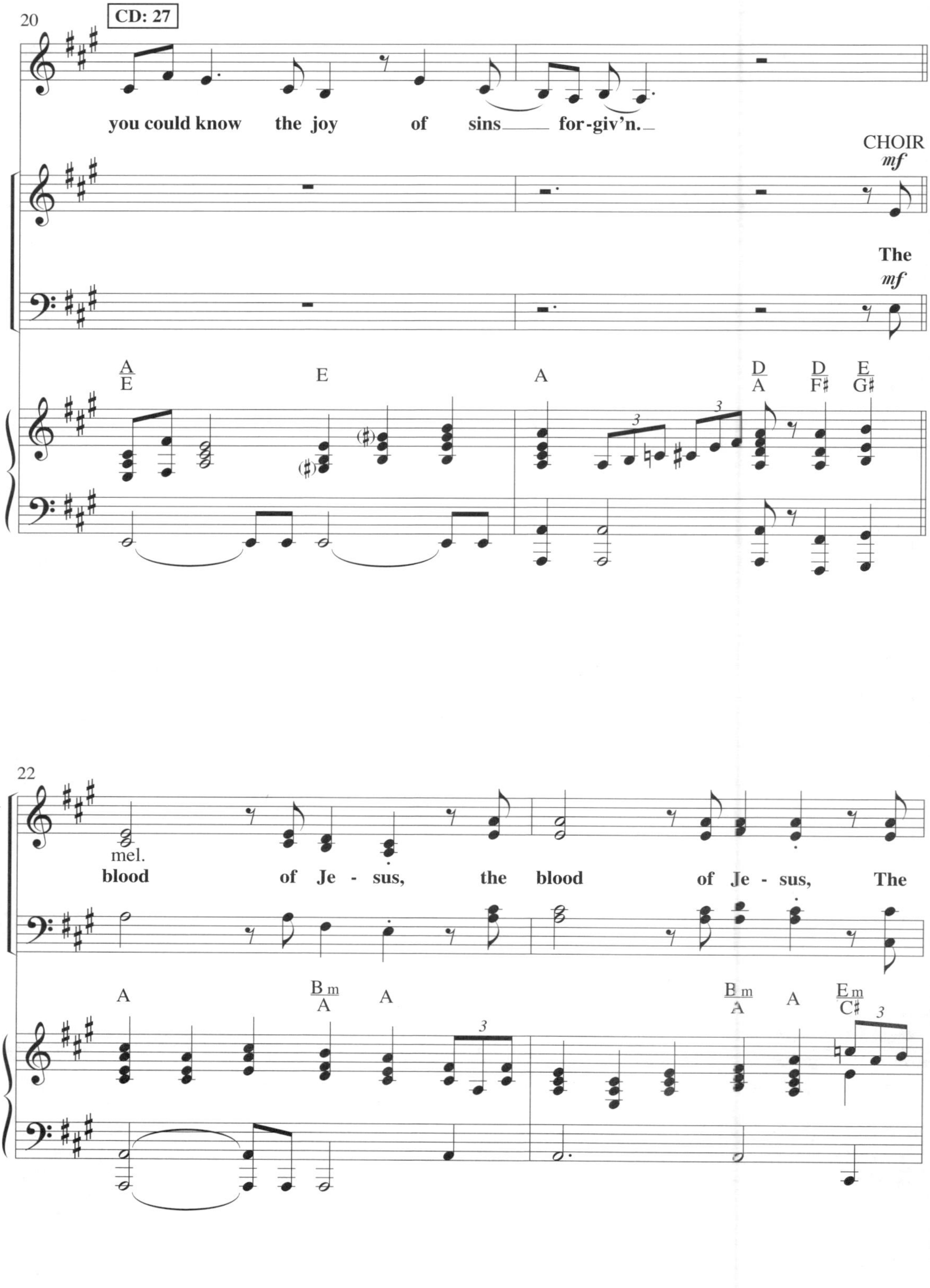

20 **CD: 27**

**you could know the joy of sins___ for-giv'n.___**

CHOIR *mf*

**The**

*mf*

A/E E A D/A D/F♯ E/G♯

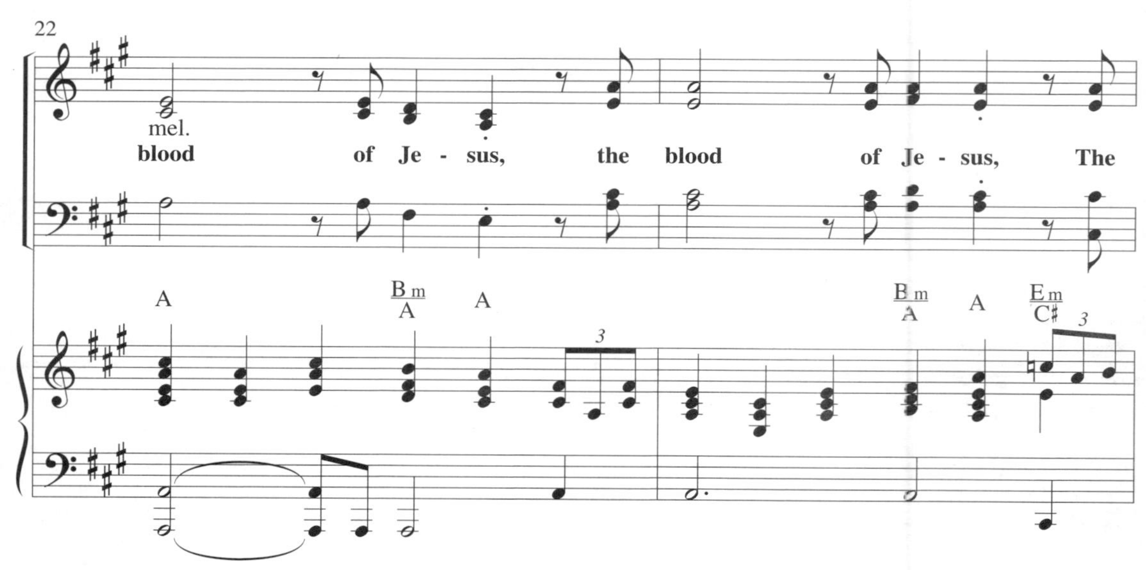

24
blood of Je - sus, can cleanse your deep - est
D
D/A
A
A/C♯
D
A/E
E
26
CD: 28
sin.
A
cresc.
A/G
D/F♯
F7sus
f
28
SOLO
f
You may have some hid - den sin,
You try to cov - er deep with - in;
And
B♭
F
Fm/D
E♭

30
ev-'ry-bod-y thinks you're life is in con - trol,
B♭/F
F
B♭
F
32
You can run but you can't hide;
God sees ev - 'ry-thing in-side,
But for -
B♭
F
Fm/D
E♭
34
CD: 29
SOLO ends
give-ness waits at the foot of Cal - va-ry's cross.
mf
The
mf
B♭/F
F
B♭
Cm7
B♭7/D

36
mel.
mel.
blood of Je - sus, the blood of Je - sus, The
E♭
Fm/E♭
E♭
Fm/E♭
E♭
E♭/G
sub. mf
38
blood of Je - sus, can cleanse your deep-est sin. The
A♭
A♭/E♭
E♭
E♭/G
A♭
E♭/B♭
B♭
E♭
A♭/C
B♭/D
40
mel.
mel.
blood of Je - sus, the blood of Je - sus, The
E♭
Fm/E♭
E♭
Fm/E♭
E♭
E♭/G

*Words by CIVILLA D. MARTIN; Music by W. STILLMAN MARTIN. Arr. © 2009 PsalmSinger Music (BMI). All rights reserved. Administered by The Copyright Company, PO Box 128139, Nashville, TN 37212-8139.

48
straight eighths
pow'r; The blood that cleans - es
G D7 G Gsus/A G/B D Dsus/E D/F♯
straight eighths
50
swing eighths
from all sin It will nev - er lose its
G Am7 G7/B C G/D B7
swing eighths
52
straight eighths
swing eighths
pow'r. It will nev - er lose its
Em G7/D C Bm7 Am7 G/D Bm/D D
straight eighths
swing eighths

OPTIONAL REPRISE

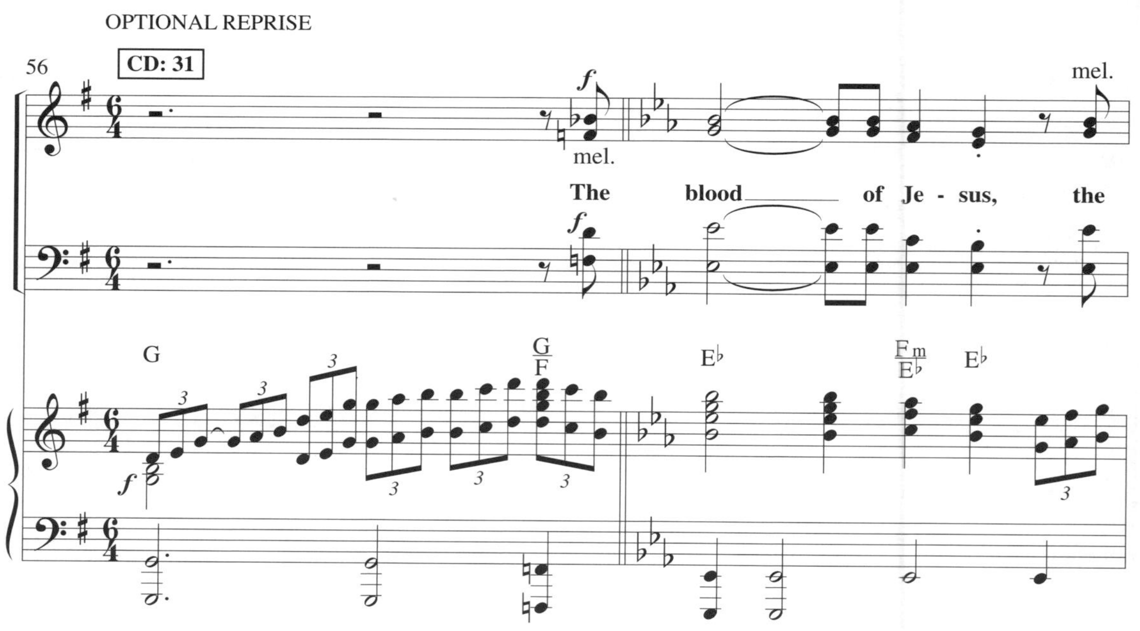

58

*straight eighths*

blood ____ of Je - sus, The blood ____ of Je - sus, can

E♭ Fm/E♭ E♭ E♭/G A♭ B♭ A♭/C B♭/D A♭/E♭ E♭ E♭/G Fm/A♭

*straight eighths*

60

*swing eighths* *straight eighths* *rit.*

cleanse your deep-est sin. O the blood can cleanse ev - 'ry

E♭/B♭ B°7 Cm E♭7/B♭ A♭ Gm7 Fm7 E♭/B♭ B♭ E♭/B♭ B♭7

*swing eighths* *straight eighths* *rit.*

63

sin. ____

E♭ A♭/E♭ E♭ E♭/B♭ E♭ E♭/B♭ E♭

8vb

# 99 1/2

Words and Music by
WAYNE HAUN
*Arr. by Wayne Haun*

7
nine and a half won't do, just won't do. Lord, I'm
D 7
A 7

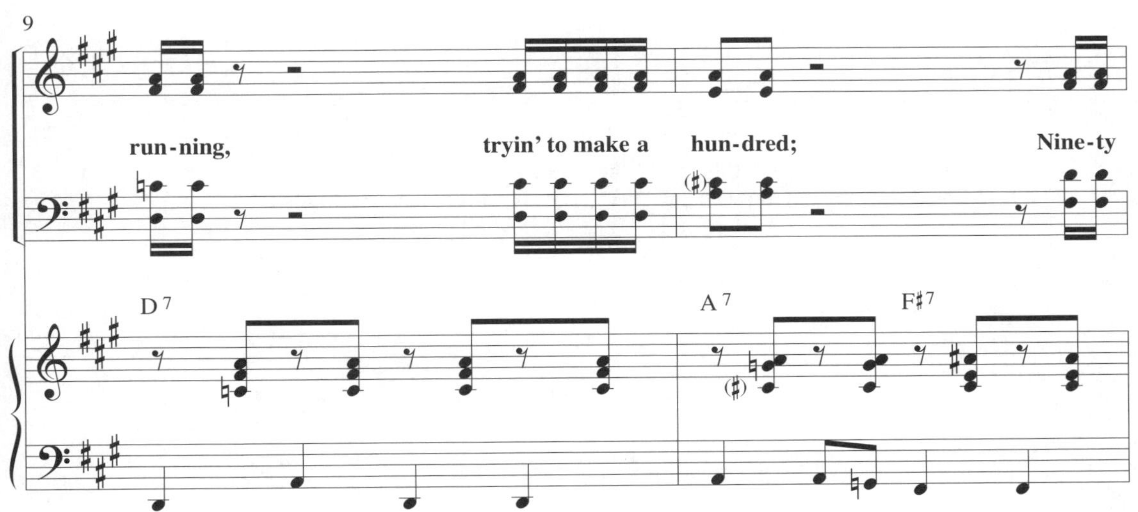
9
run-ning, tryin' to make a hun-dred; Nine-ty
D 7
A 7
F♯7

CD: 33 1st time
CD: 35 2nd time
CD: 37 3rd time
11
3rd time to Coda
TRIO unis.
f
1. I
2. Now
nine and a half won't do, just won't do.
B 7
D
E
A
D 7
A
G
3rd time to Coda
13
SOLO 1
f
glad - ly start - ed on this race the day I met the Lord;
I won't get dis - cour - aged if I stum - ble or fall down;
I
A 7
C
D
15
SOLO 2
f
prom - ised Him my all and He made heav - en my re - ward.
God will pick me up and put my feet back on the ground.
O
See
A 7
A 7
C♯

17

SOLO 3

*f*

He has been so faith - ful to give strength for ev - 'ry - day; Now I've
He's been known to leave the fold to claim one of His own; But I

CHOIR *div.*

Oo.

D 7 D 7/F♯ G 13 G♯13

CD: 34 *1st time*

CD: 36 *2nd time*

19

TRIO *parts* *f*

1

(to pg. 60, meas. 5)

come so far and I in - tend to make it all the way.
wan - na stay so close to Him as I

1

(to pg. 60, meas. 5)

*f*

Lord, I'm

*f*

A 7

1

(to pg. 60, meas. 5)

E A D/E

21
2
(to pg. 60, meas. 5)
CODA
TRIO *parts*
SOLO 1
keep trav-'ling on.
Fif - teen, twen - ty, twen - ty five, Is
Lord, I'm
E
A
D
E
A 7
23
SOLO 2
just a start but keep on try-in'.
Thir - ty, for - ty, fif - ty two, Is
A 7
G M7
A
25
SOLO 3
just half way keep press-ing thro'.
Six - ty, se-ven-ty, eigh - ty nine, And
B♭7

27

get-ting close don't fall be-hind.

*f*

Nin - ty, one, two, three, four, five, I'm

*f*

Nin - ty, one, two, three, four, five, I'm

*f*

B♭7 C7 C7/E

CD: 38

29

gon - na cross that fin - ish line.

gon - na cross that fin - ish line. Lord, I'm

F7 E♭/F

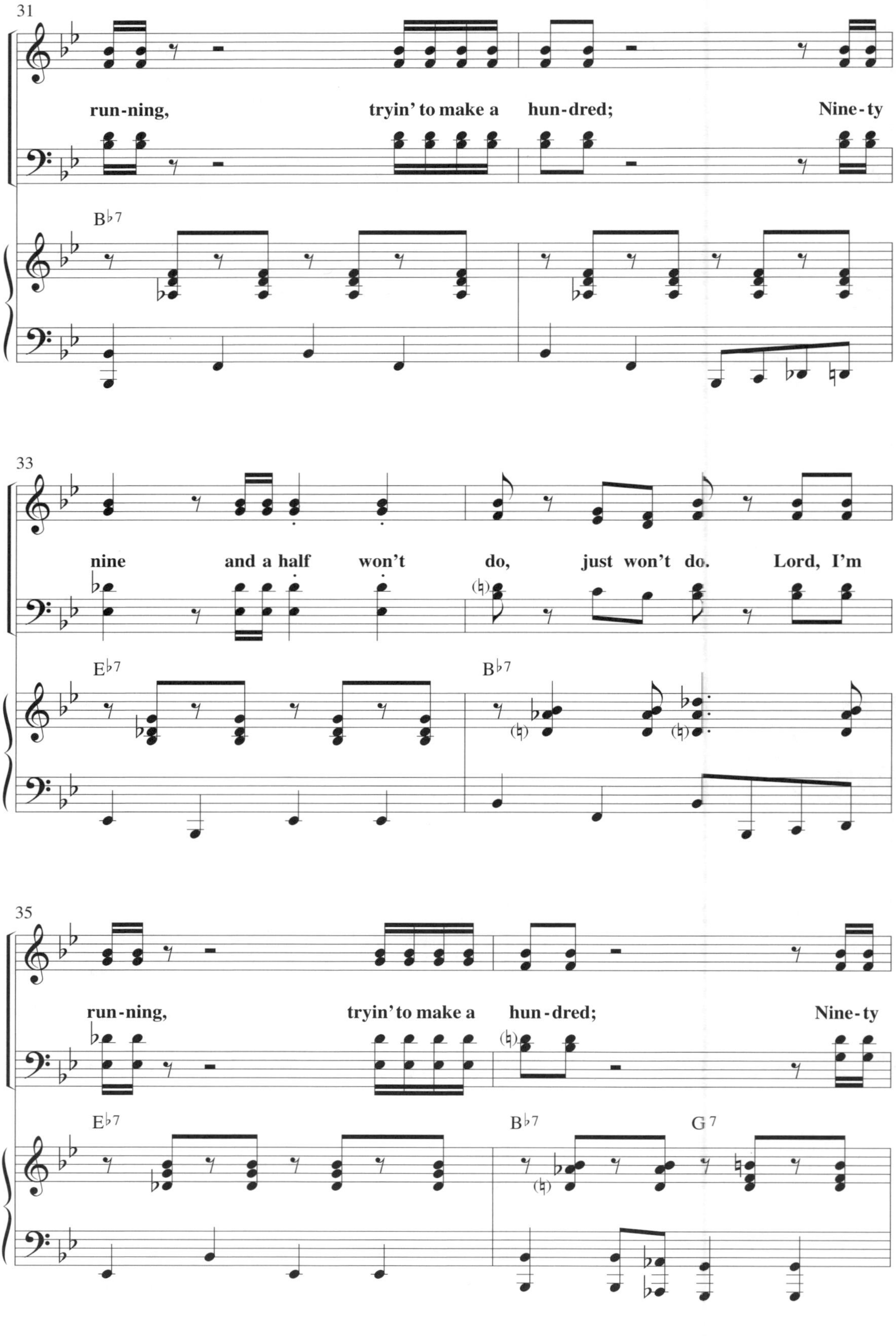
31
run-ning, tryin' to make a hun-dred; Nine-ty
B♭7
33
nine and a half won't do, just won't do. Lord, I'm
E♭7
B♭7
35
run-ning, tryin' to make a hun-dred; Nine-ty
E♭7
B♭7
G7

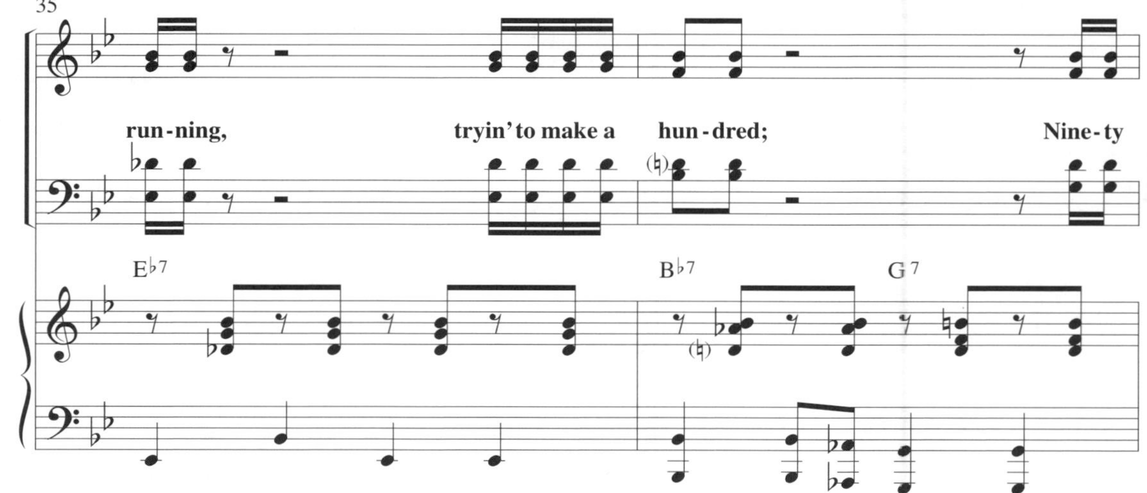

CD: 39
nine and a half won't do, just won't do. O Lord, I'm
C7 E♭/F B♭ E♭7 B♭ A♭
run-ning, tryin' to make a hun-dred; Nine-ty
B♭7
nine and a half won't do, just won't do. Lord, I'm
E♭7 B♭7

43
running,
tryin' to make a
hundred;
Nine-ty
E♭7
B♭7
G7
45
rit.
nine
and a
half
won't
do,
just
won't
C7
E♭/F
B♭
E♭7
rit.
47
a tempo
do.
B♭
N.C.
a tempo

# We Speak Your Name

Words and Music by
JASON CLARK
*Arr. by Wayne Haun*

10
that there is no end. When our
A♭/E♭
B♭sus
B♭
G m7

12
heart is torn, our faith is worn, And friends are hard to find. We
C m
G/B
E♭/B♭
F 7

CD: 41
14
speak Your name, O pre - cious Lord, You bring peace
F m7
E♭/G
A♭

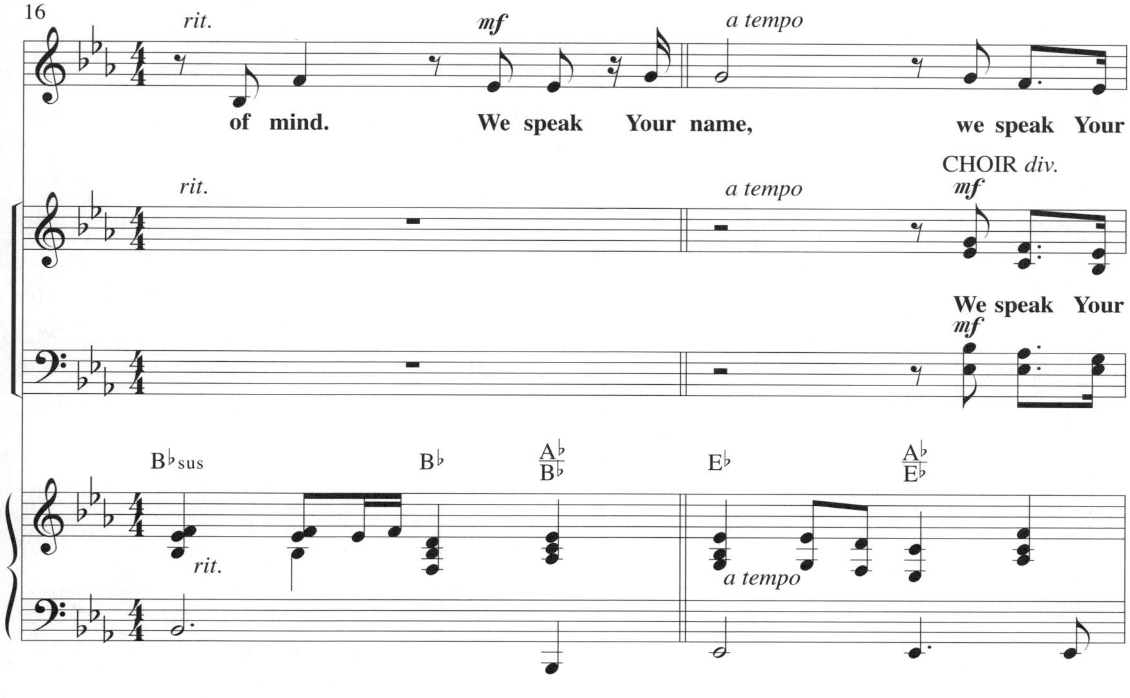

16
rit.
mf
a tempo
of mind. We speak Your name, we speak Your
CHOIR div.
rit.
a tempo
mf
We speak Your
mf
B♭sus
B♭
A♭/B♭
E♭
A♭/E♭
rit.
a tempo

18
name, In times of joy, in times of
name, In times of joy, in times of
E♭
B♭/D
Cm
A♭

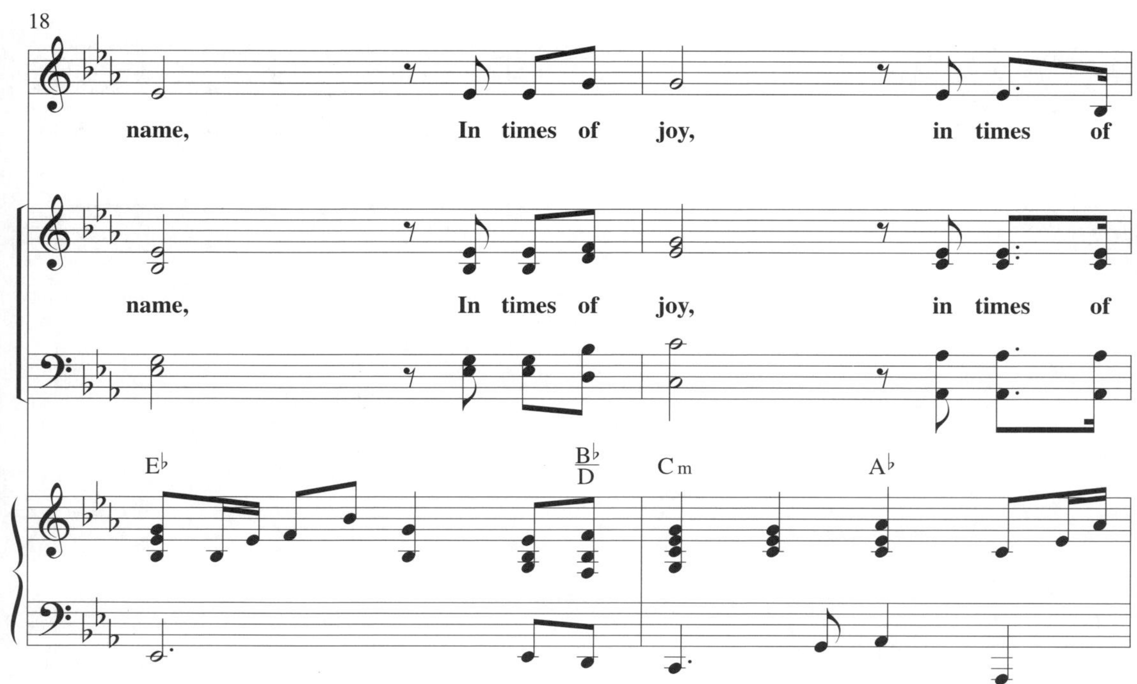

20

pain; We speak Your name, We speak Your

pain; We speak Your name, We speak Your

B♭sus B♭ Gm7 Cm

22

CD: 42

name In sun - shine or rain, we speak Your

name In sun - shine or rain, we speak Your

A♭ E♭/G Fm A♭ E♭/G B♭ A♭/B♭

24
name.
The doc - tor gives no hope, "We've
name.
E♭
B♭/E♭
26
done all we can do." And times are hard, mon - ey's short,
A♭/E♭
E♭
B♭/E♭
28
and the bills are due. When your
f
A♭/E♭
B♭sus
B♭
G m7
cresc.

30
strength is gone, the days seem long, You feel like giv - ing in. Just
Cm
G/B
E♭/B♭
F7
f
32
speak the name of our God, You'll find strength
CD: 43
Fm7
E♭/G
A♭
34
rit.
in Him. We speak
a tempo
Your name, we speak Your
We speak Your
f
B♭sus
B♭
A♭/B♭
E♭
A♭/E♭

36

name, In times of joy, in times of

name, In times of joy, in times of

E♭ B♭/D Cm A♭

38

pain; We speak Your name, We speak Your

pain; We speak Your name, We speak Your

B♭sus B♭ Gm7 Cm

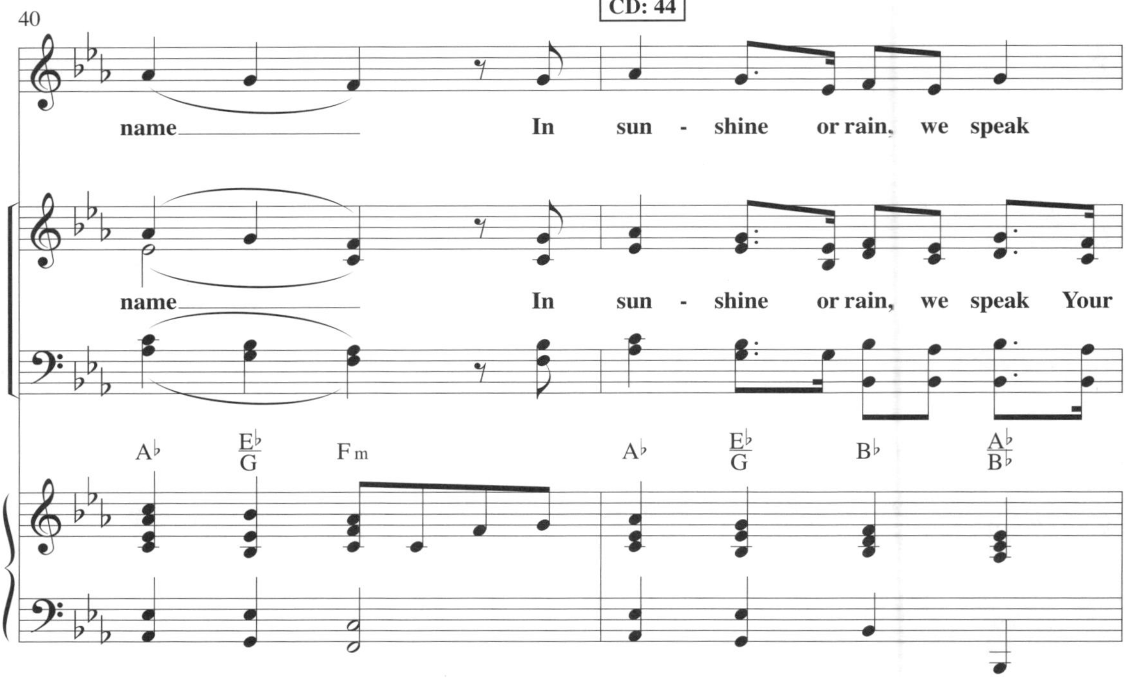

40
CD: 44
name In sun - shine or rain, we speak
name In sun - shine or rain, we speak Your
A♭ E♭/G Fm A♭ E♭/G B♭ A♭/B♭

42
ff
Your name. My rock, my shield, my hid - ing place, My
f
name. We speak Your
f
E♭ F/E♭

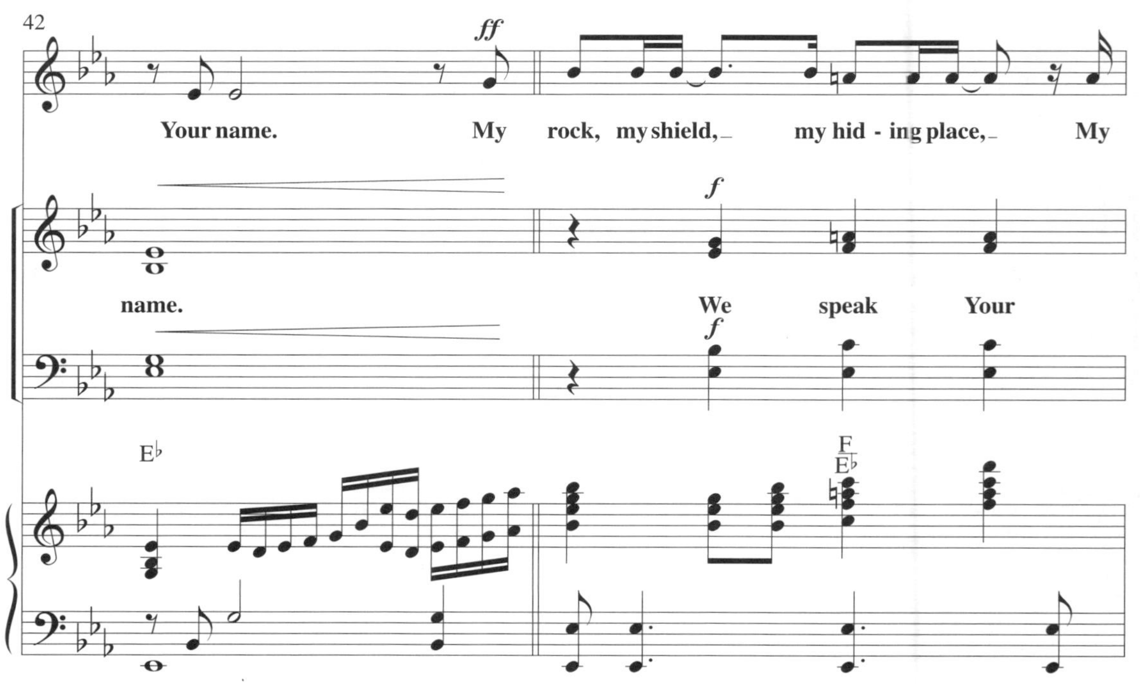

44

bound-less store of grace; My Lord, my life, my way, my end, My

name, we speak Your

D♭/E♭ A♭/E♭ E♭ E♭ F/E♭

46

CD: 45

Sav - ior and my friend, my

name, my Friend, my

D♭/E♭ B♭sus

*cresc.*

48 *rit.* *a tempo*

friend. We speak Your name, we speak Your

*rit.* *ff* *a tempo*

Friend. We speak Your name, we speak Your

*ff*

B sus A/B E A/E

*ff rit.* *a tempo*

50

name, In times of joy, in times of

mel.

name In times of joy, in times of

E B/D♯ C♯m A

52

pain; We speak Your name, We speak Your

pain; We speak Your name, We speak Your

B sus B G♯m7 C♯m

CD: 46

54

name In sun - shine or rain, we speak

mel.

name In sun - shine or rain, we speak Your

A E/G♯ F♯m A E/G♯ B A/B

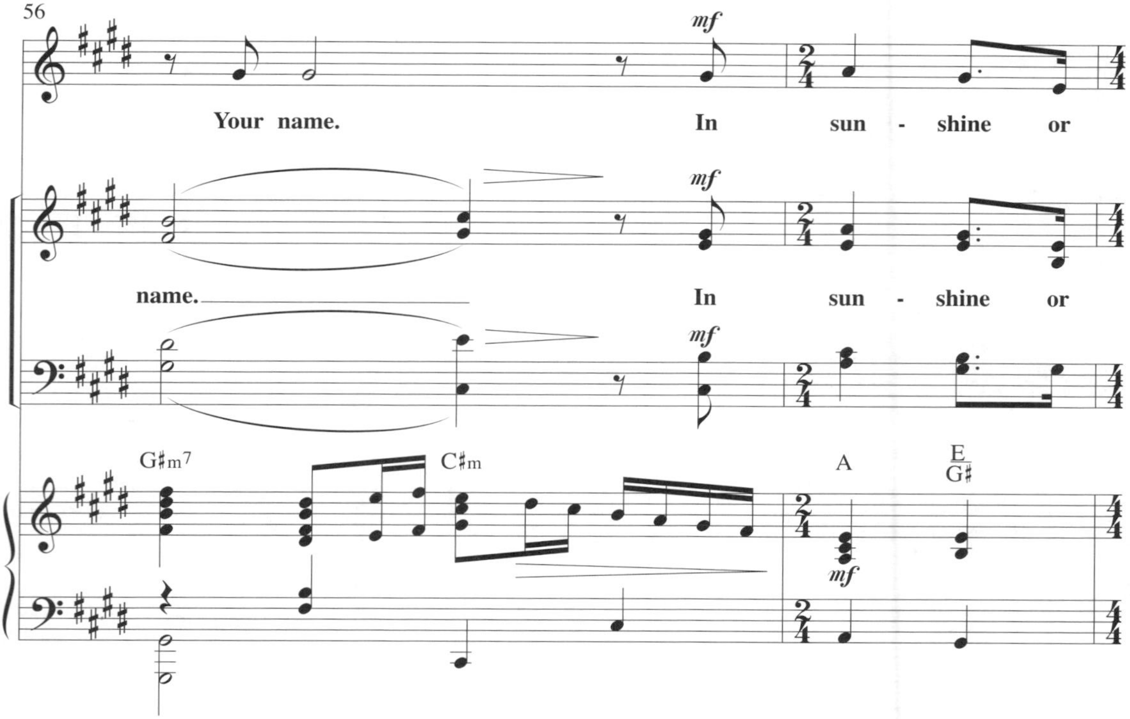

56
mf
Your name.
In sun - shine or
mf
name.
In sun - shine or
mf
G♯m7
C♯m
A
E
G♯
mf

58
mp
rain,
we speak
dim.
rain,
dim.
B sus
B
dim.

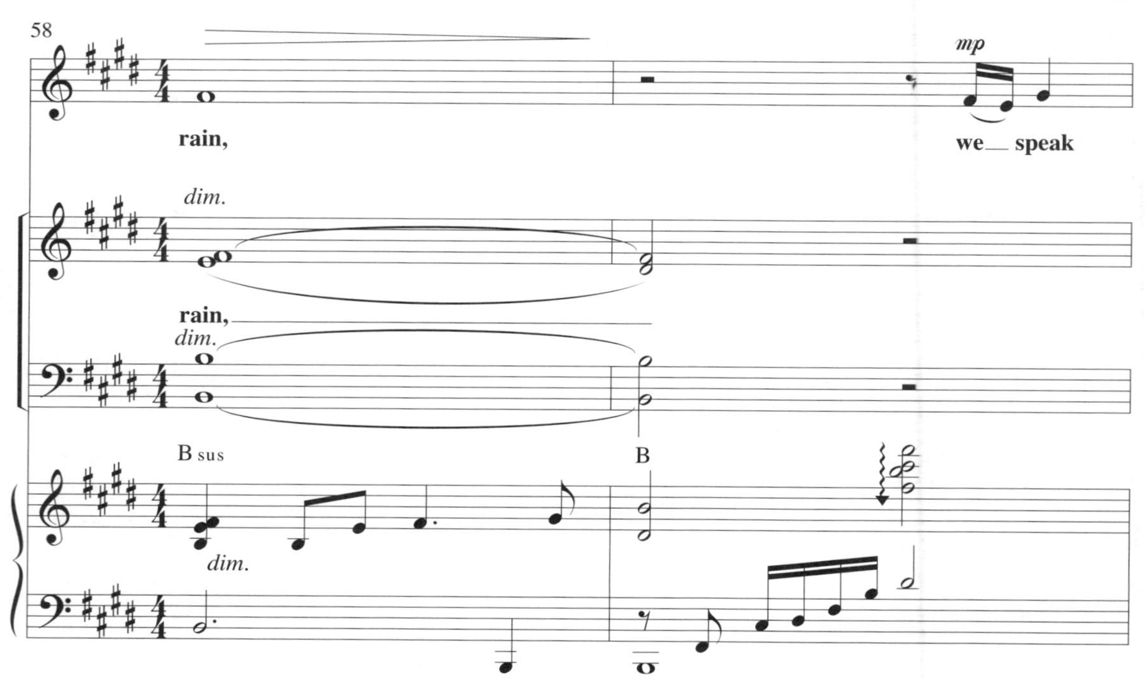

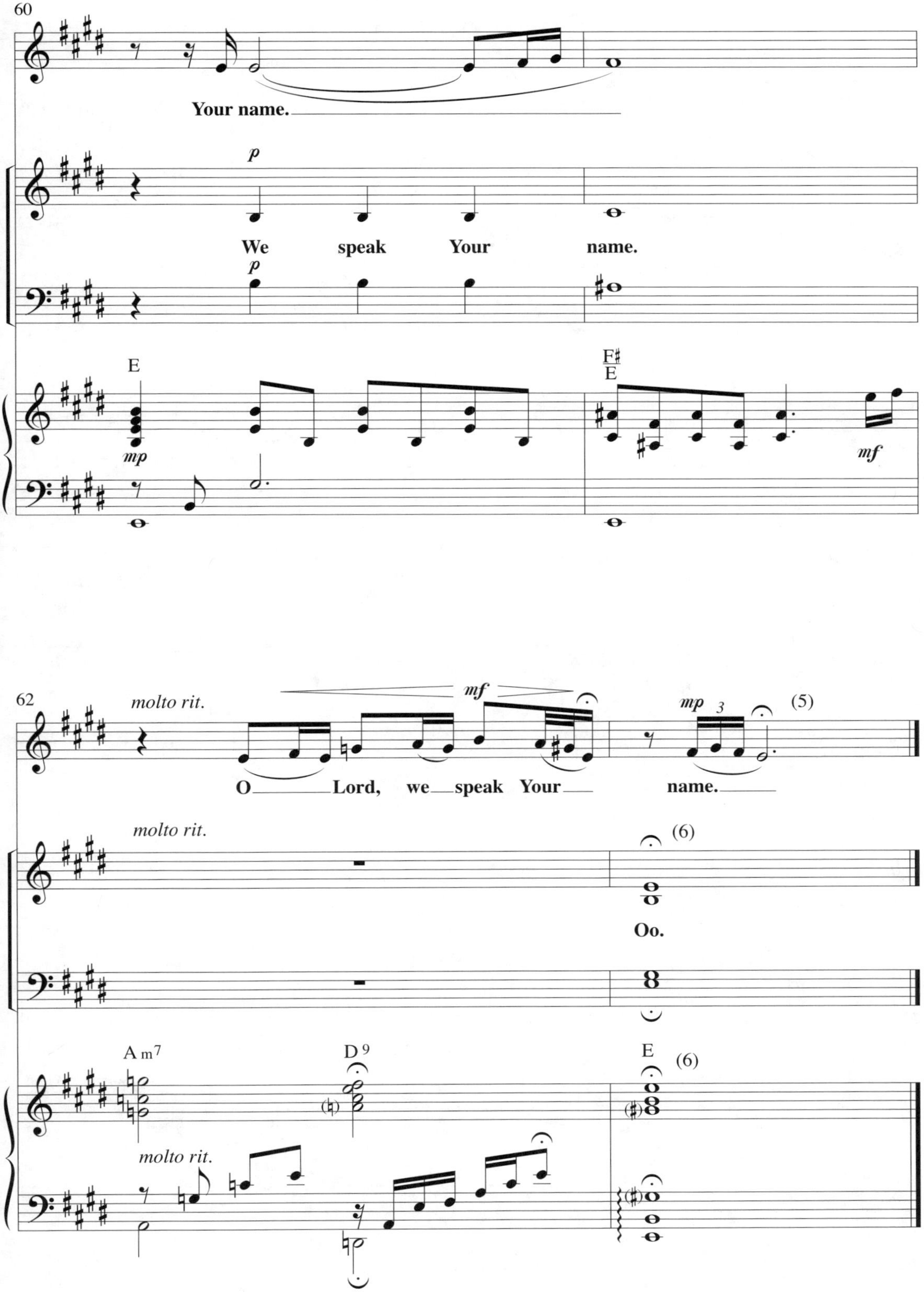

62

*molto rit.*

*mf*

*mp* 3 (5)

O Lord, we speak Your name.

*molto rit.*

(6)

Oo.

Am7 D9 E (6)

(♮) (♯)

*molto rit.*

(♯)

# Born to Climb

Words and Music by
WAYNE HAUN and
JOEL LINDSEY
*Arr. by Wayne Haun*

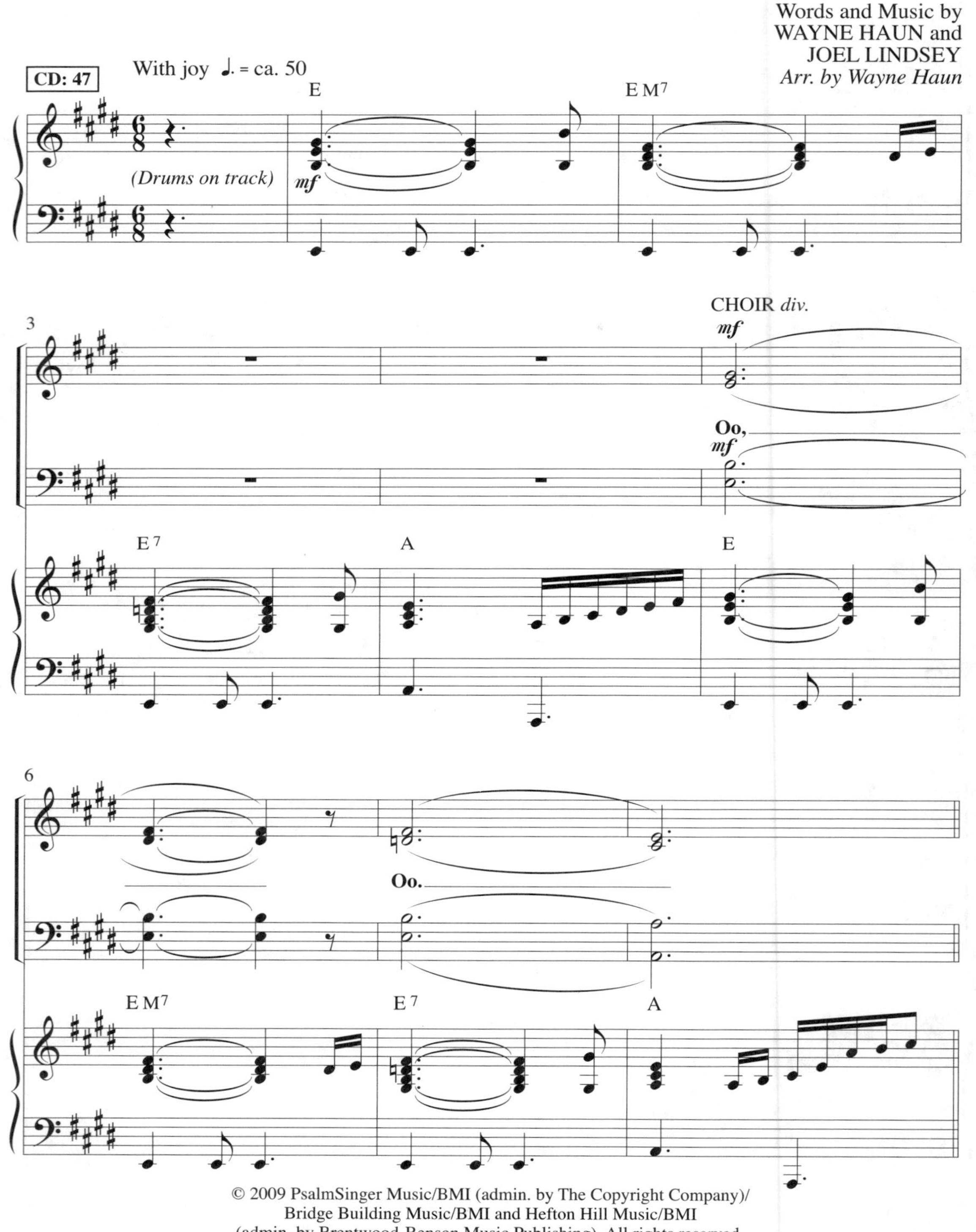

9
SOLO
mf
1. Right now you feel like you'd ra - ther be an - y - where else
SOLO
mf
2. God has not giv - en a spir - it of fear or a
E
EM7
mf
11
than here where you are; 'Cause
bur - den that you can - not bear;
E7
A
CD: 48 1st time
CD: 50 2nd time
13
life has a way of ar - rang - ing your plans and the
Just at the mo - ment you feel hope is fad - in' be -
F♯m7
E
G♯

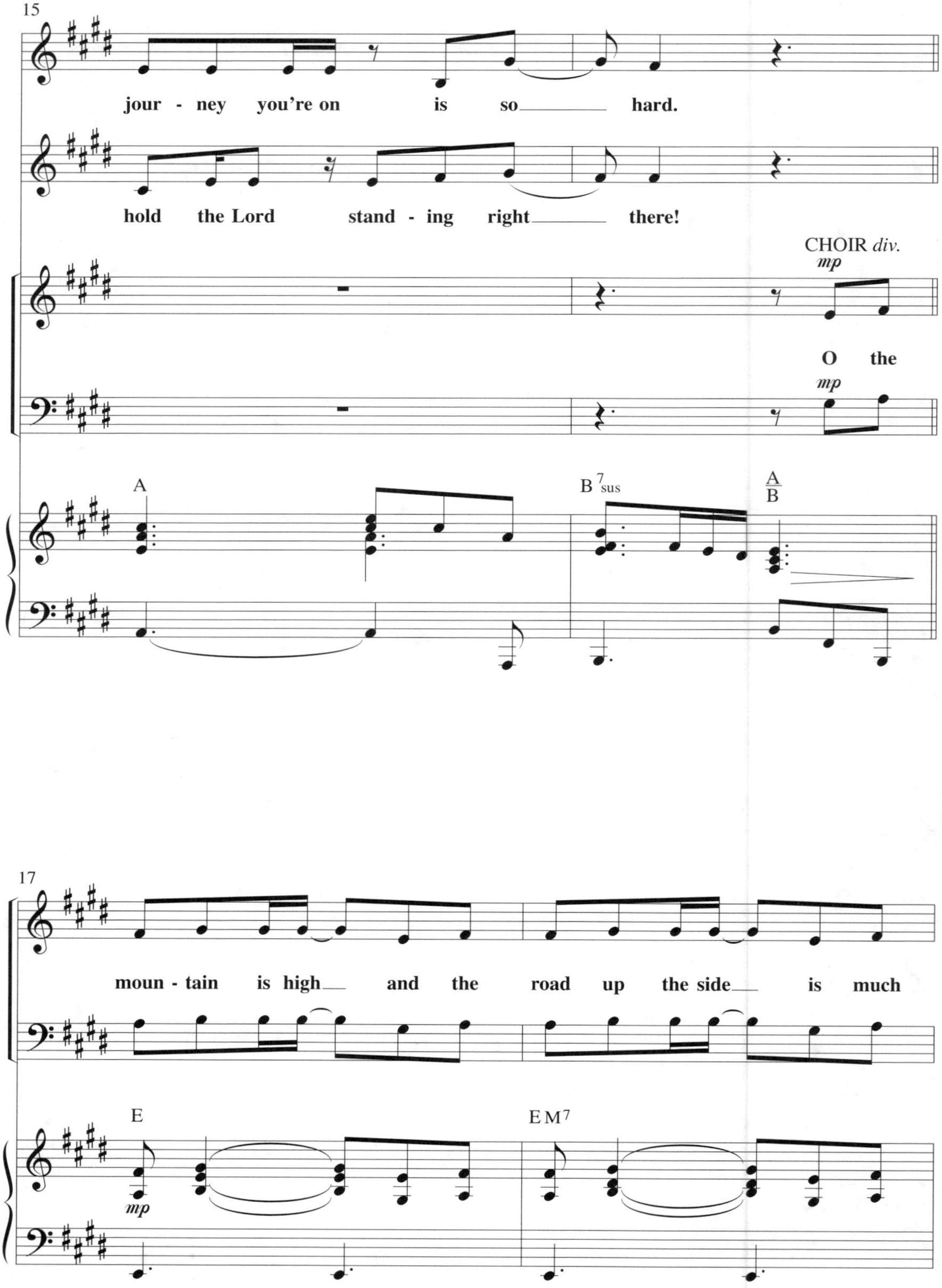

15

jour - ney you're on is so hard.

hold the Lord stand - ing right there!

CHOIR *div.*

*mp*

O the

*mp*

A

B 7sus

A/B

19
steep - er than you thought it'd be; And
E7
A
21
you're out of breath and you're scared half to death that you
E
EM7
23
won't have the faith to be - lieve;
E7
A

DUET

25

*f*

Grace, ___ sweet grace, ___ has

*mf*

Grace, grace,

*mf*

E B m7

*f*

27

strength - ened you time af - ter time, So

strength - ened you time af - ter time, So

A E

29

CD: 51 *2nd time*

don't be a-fraid of the moun - tain 'cause

don't be a-fraid of the moun - tain 'cause

A E/G♯ A

31

1

CD: 49

friend you were born to climb.

friend you were born to climb.

E/B B7 E EM7

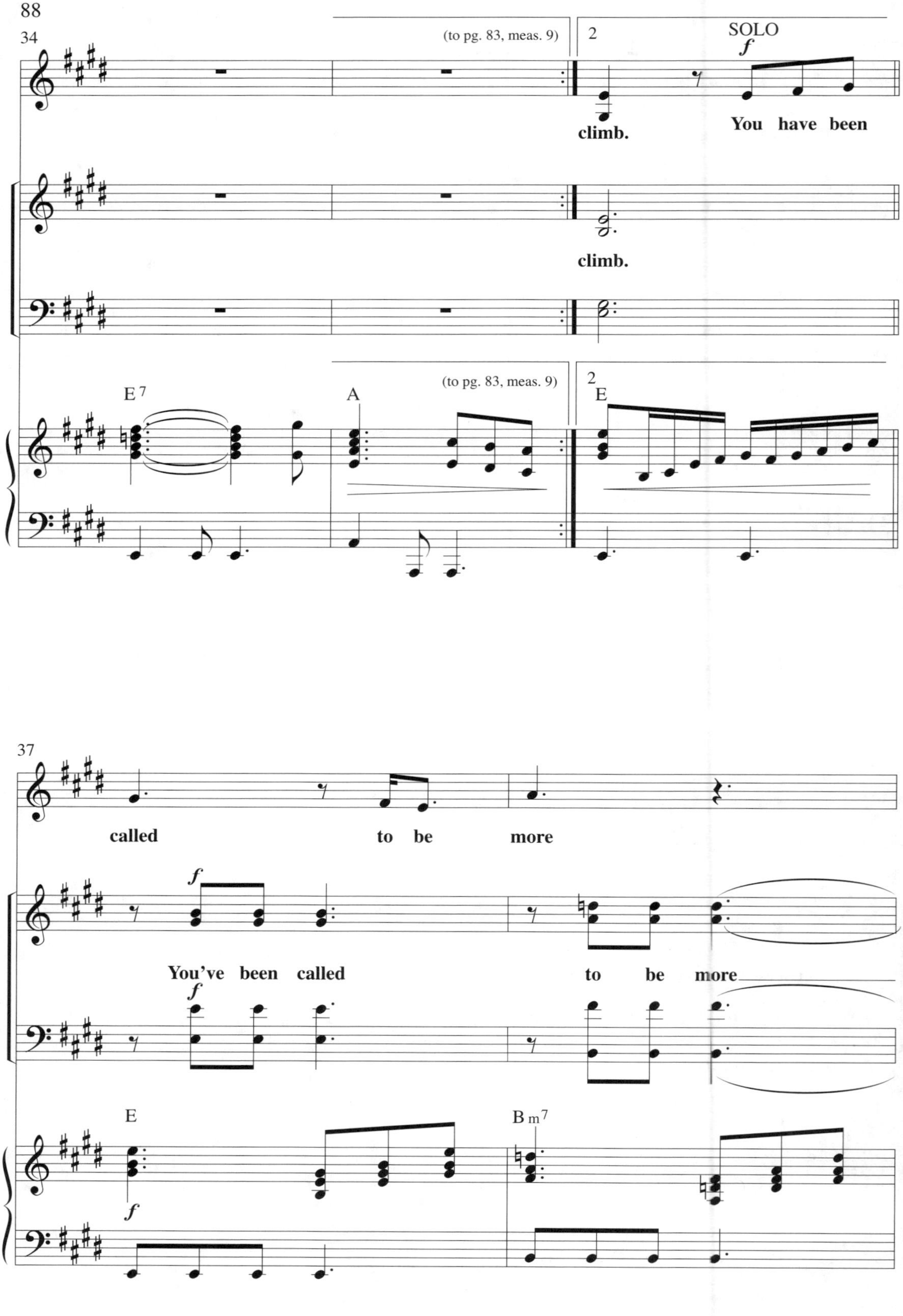

34

(to pg. 83, meas. 9)

2

SOLO

*f*

climb. You have been

climb.

E7 A

(to pg. 83, meas. 9)

2

E

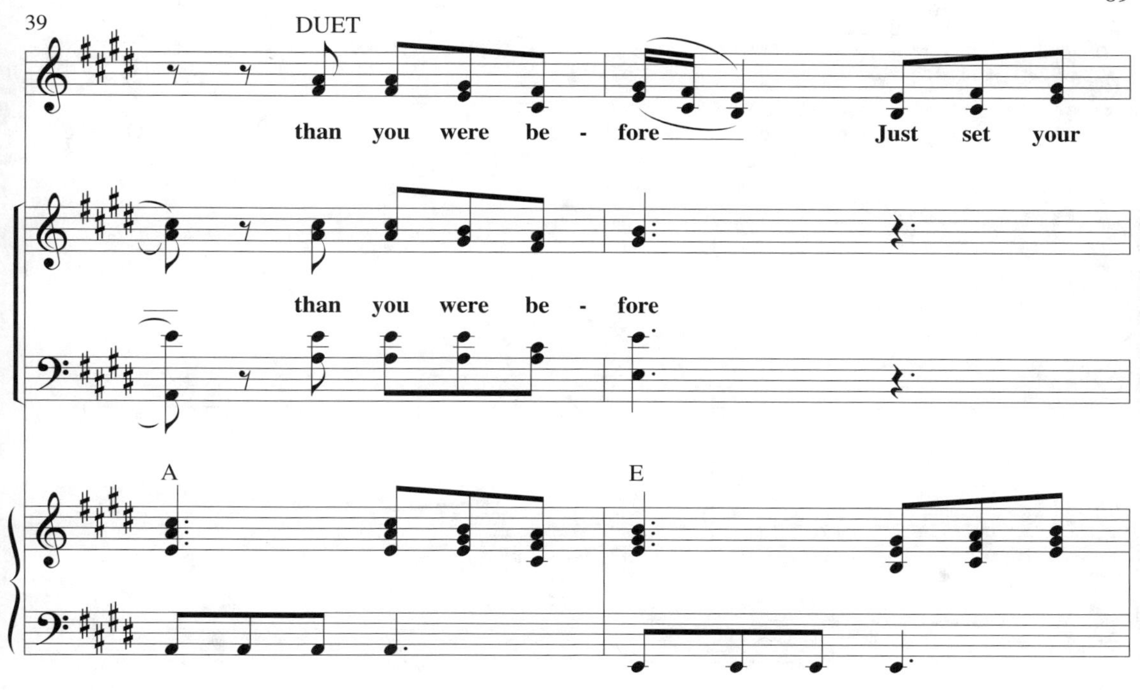
39
DUET
than you were be - fore
Just set your
than you were be - fore
A
E

41
sights
on Heav - en - ly
heights
Set your sights on heav - en - ly heights,
E
B m7

43
CD: 52
SOLO
mp
and trust in the Lord. O the
mf
trust in the Lord.
mf
A
B sus
B
A/B
46
mountain is high and the road up the side is much
E
E M7
mp
48
steep - er than you thought it'd be;
E7
A

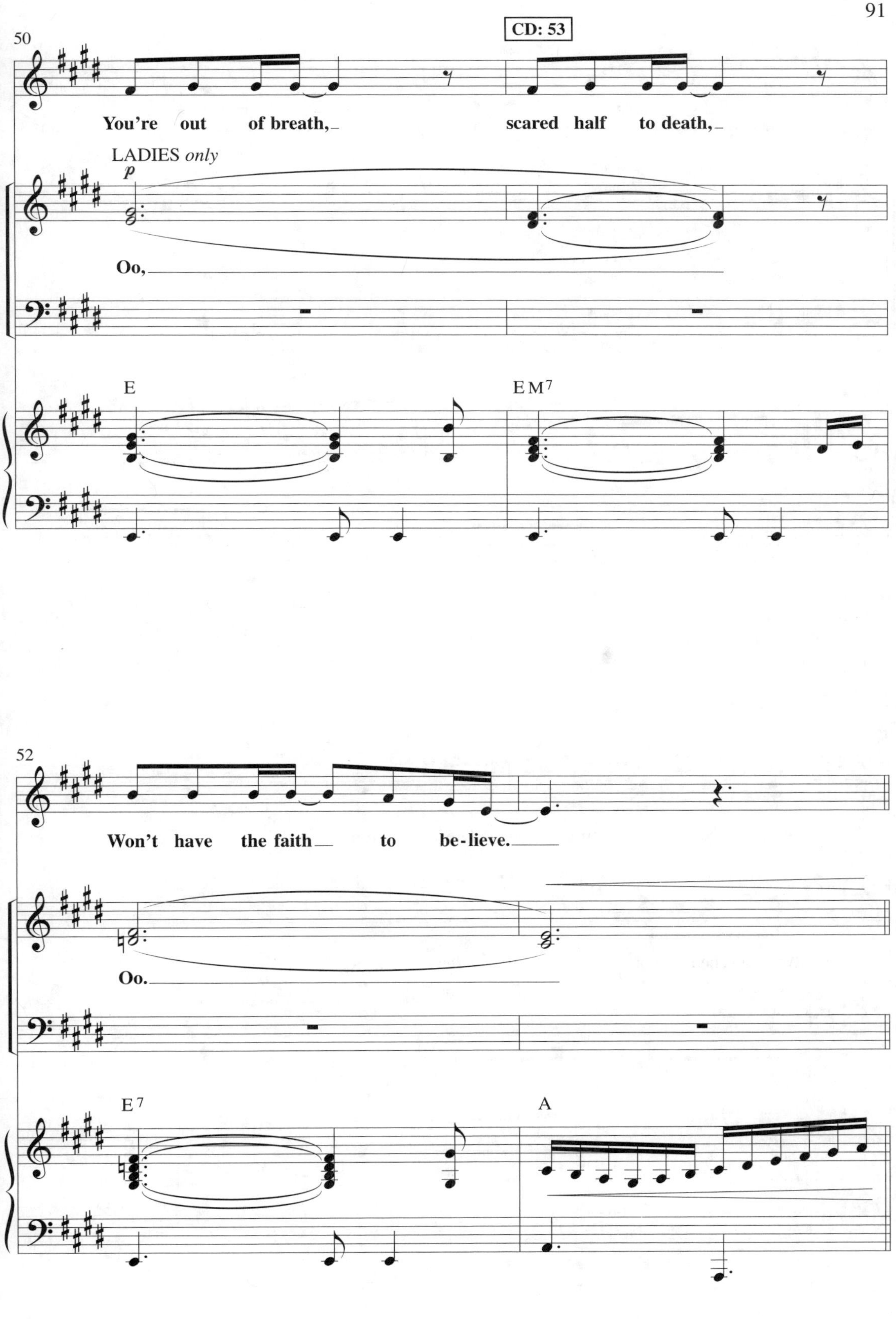

CD: 53

50

You're out of breath, scared half to death,

LADIES *only*

*p*

Oo,

E

EM7

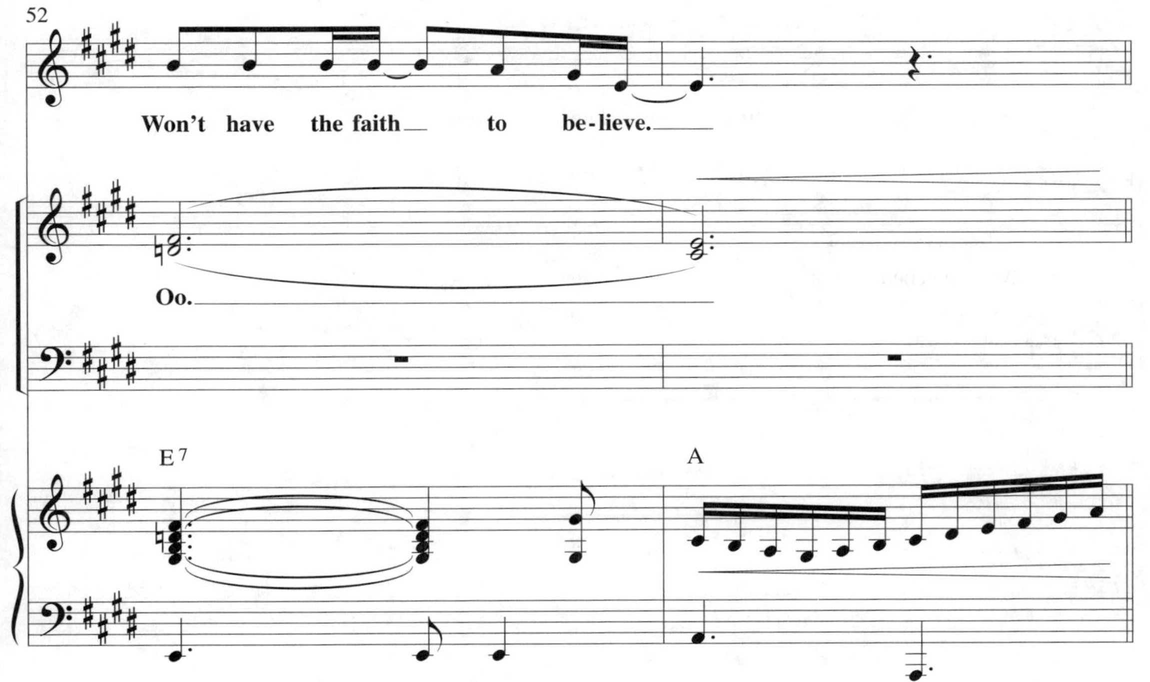

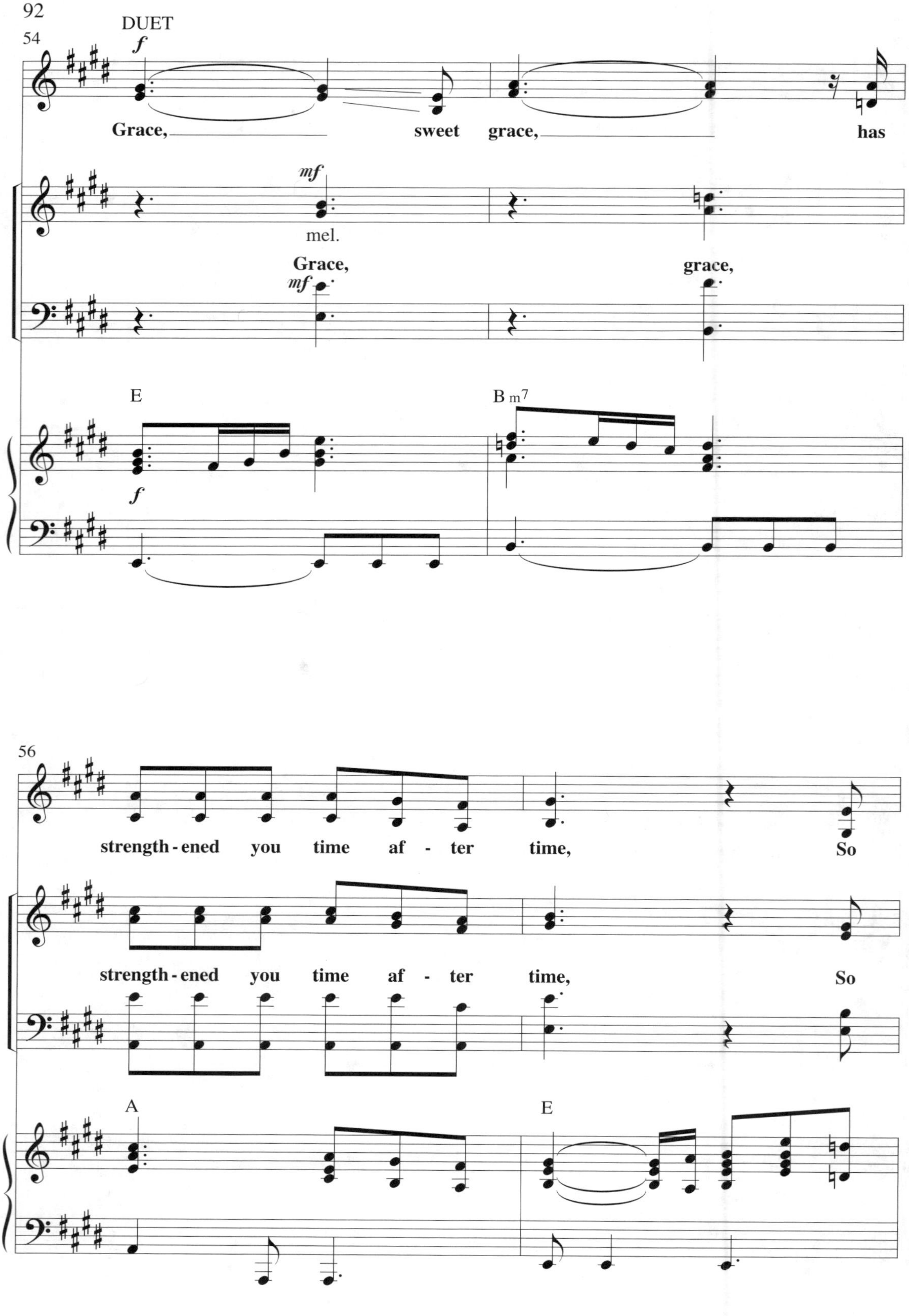

DUET

54

*f*

Grace, sweet grace, has

*mf*

mel.

Grace, grace,

*mf*

E

B m7

*f*

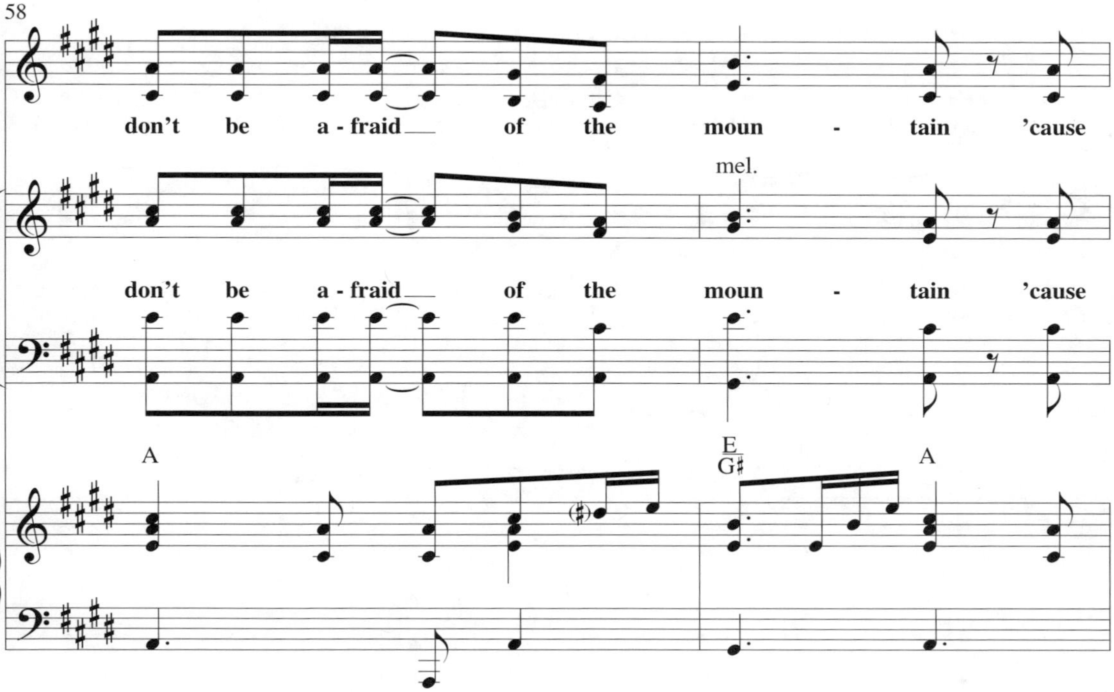
58
don't be a - fraid of the moun - tain 'cause
mel.
don't be a - fraid of the moun - tain 'cause
A
E/G♯
A

60
friend you were born to climb. So
friend you were born to climb. So
E/B
B 7
E

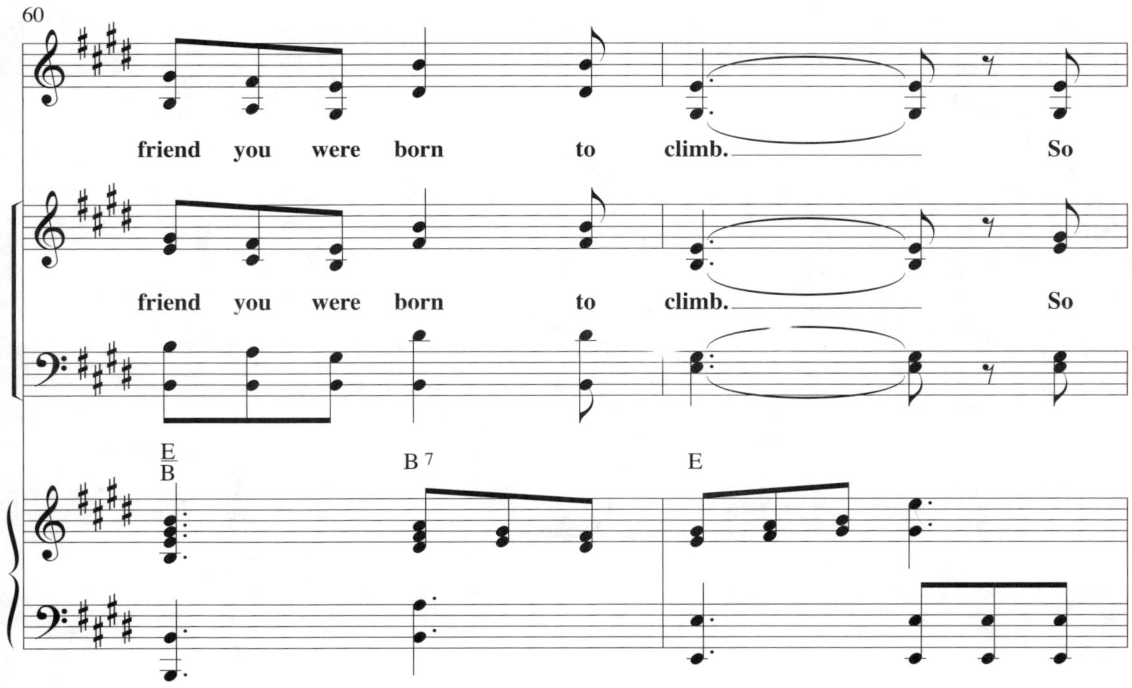

62

don't be a-fraid of the moun - tain 'cause

don't be a-fraid of the moun - tain 'cause

A E/G♯ A

64

friend you were born to climb,

friend you were born to climb,

E/B B7 E

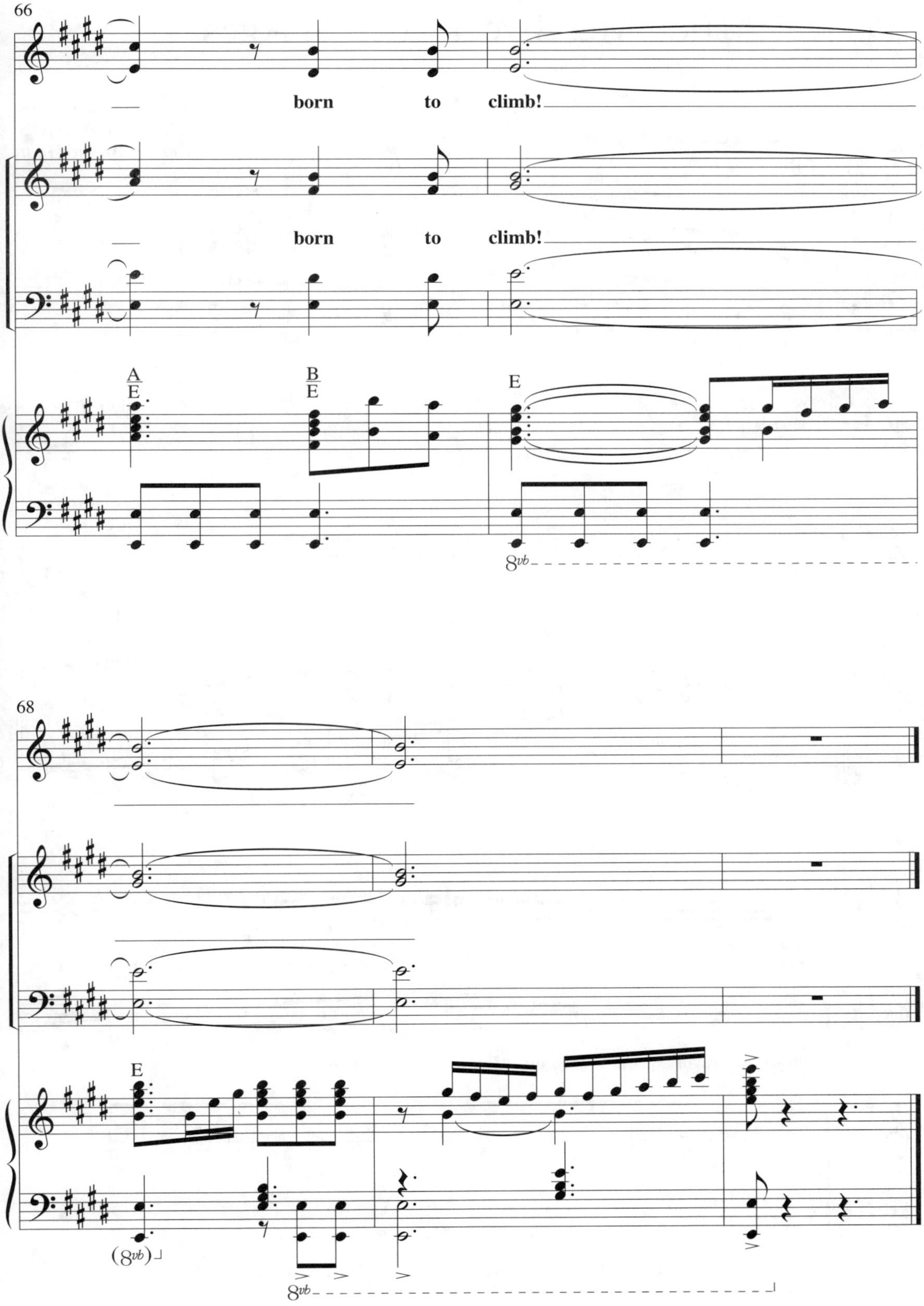

66

born to climb!

born to climb!

A/E B/E E

8vb

68

E

(8vb)

8vb

# Hide Me, Sweet Rock of Ages

Words and Music by
NANCY HARMON
*Arr. by Wayne Haun*

6
shel - ter in the time of storm;
He's a
bright and the Morn - ing Star;
He's the
D
A
7
sure foun - da - tion, He's a cor - ner - stone,
an
Liv - ing Wa - ter, He's the Bread of Life,
He's a
A
A
C♯
8
an - chor for the wear - y soul.
If you're
song for a bro - ken heart;
He's a
B 7
E 7

9
seek - in' shel - ter from the storms a - round you and you
lov - ing Sav - ior, He's the Lamb of God, Lord of
A
CD: 55 1st time
CD: 57 2nd time
10
need new strength to en - dure;
Ah, step up
lords and King of kings;
He's a
D6
C♯°7
B m
11
on His prom - ise, He's a Rock of A - ges and His sav - ing pow'r is
faith-ful Fa - ther watch-in' o - ver His chil - dren, Nev-er slum-bers, nev - er
A
F♯m
A
E
E7

sure.
SOLO both times
sleeps. Just cry hide me till the
CHOIR div.
Hide me, sweet Rock of A - ges,
A
E
14
storms, I want You to hide
Till the storms of life are past;
Hide me, sweet
D
A
E

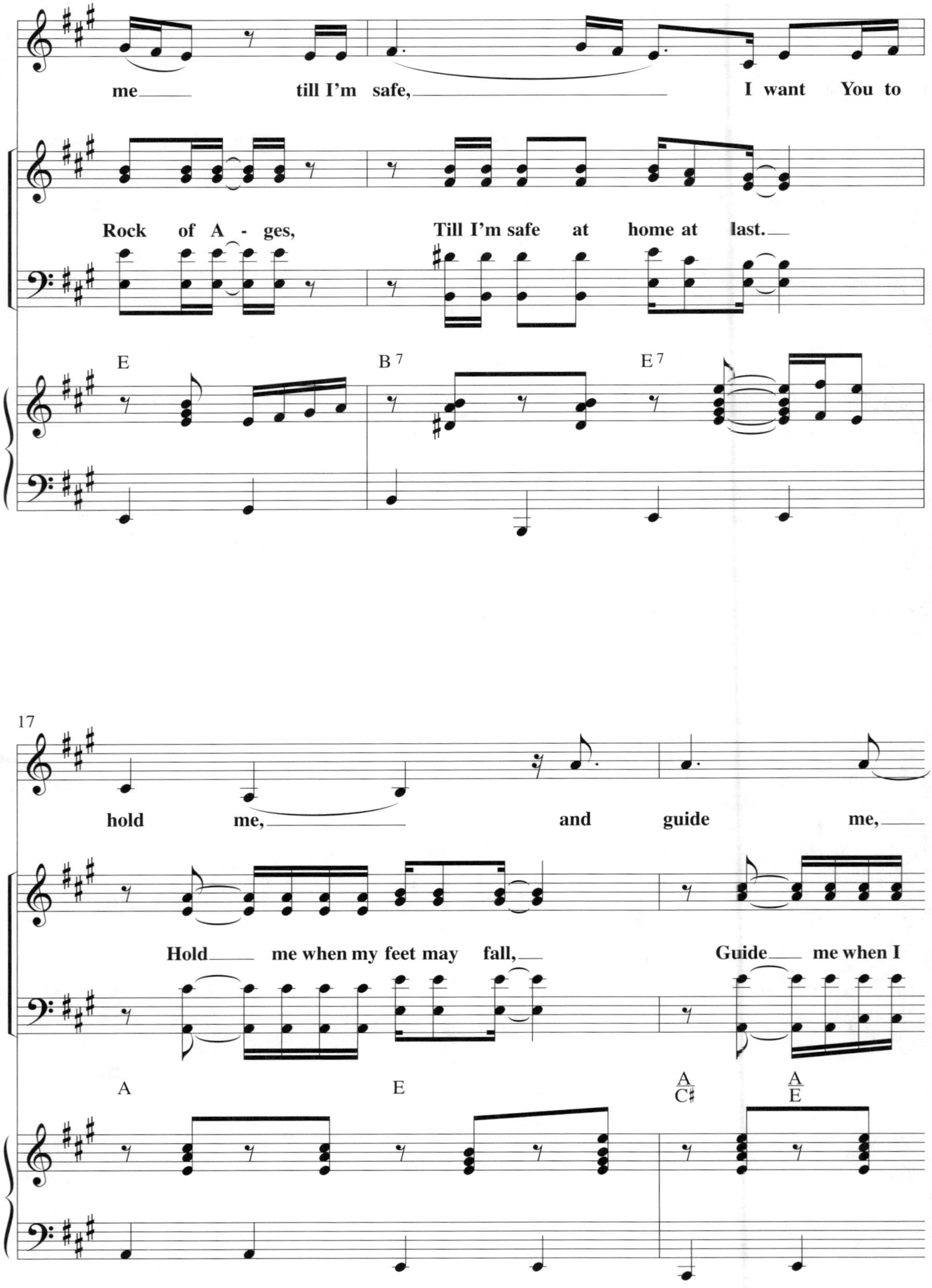

17

hold me, and guide me,

Hold me when my feet may fall, Guide me when I

A E A/C♯ A/E

CD: 58 *2nd time*

O sweet Rock of A-ges, let me

can-not see, O sweet Rock of A - ges, let me

D A F♯m

20

CD: 56 *1st time*

1

hide my - self in Thee.

hide my - self in Thee.

A/E E7

1 N.C.

22

(to pg.96, meas. 5) 2

2. He's a

*mp*

Sweet Rock of A -

*mp*

A (to pg.96, meas. 5) 2 A

24

*mf*

He's a shel - ter in the time of storm.

- ges,

*mf*

Sweet Rock of A -

*mf*

A D/A A

*mp*

26

*f*

Sure Foun - da - tion, the Cor - ner - stone.

- ges,

*f*

Sweet Rock of A -

A D/A A

28

*ff*

O He's an an - chor for the wear - y soul.

- ges,

*mf*

O

A D/A A

30

Sweet Rock of A -

*f*

sweet, sweet Rock of A - ges, Sweet, sweet Rock of A -

*f*

Bm F♯/C♯ D A/E Bm F♯/C♯ D A/E

CD: 59

- ges.

*f*

Let me

- ges, Sweet Rock of A - ges, Let me

A/E Bm F♯/C♯ D6

33

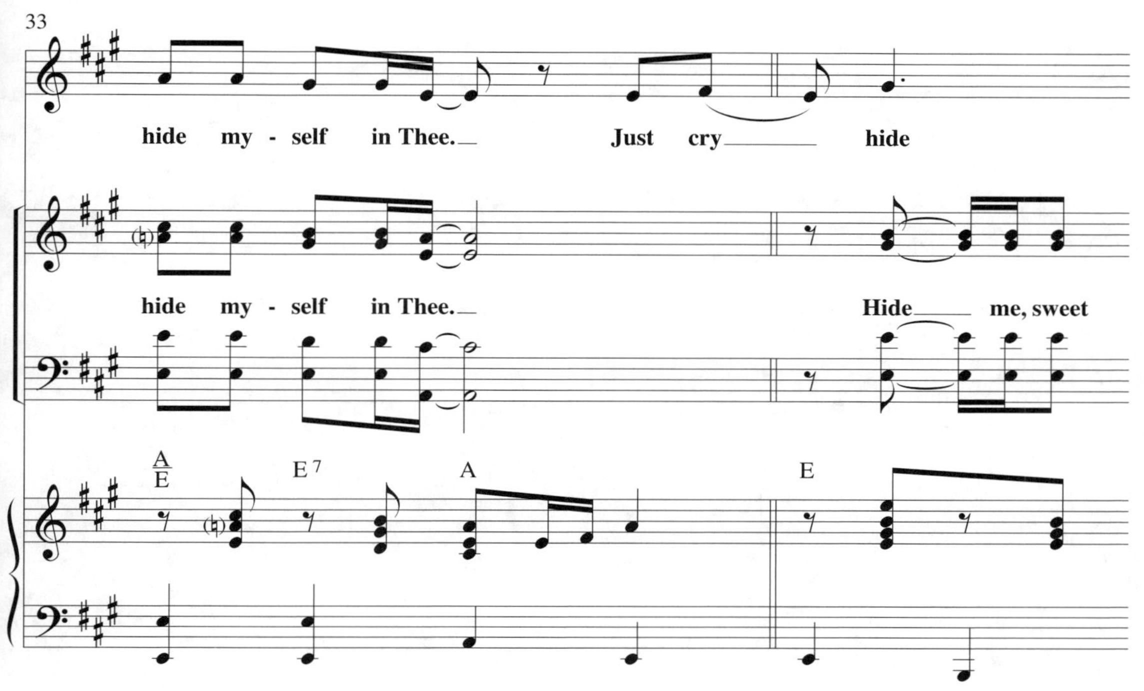
hide my - self in Thee. Just cry hide
hide my - self in Thee. Hide me, sweet
A/E E7 A E

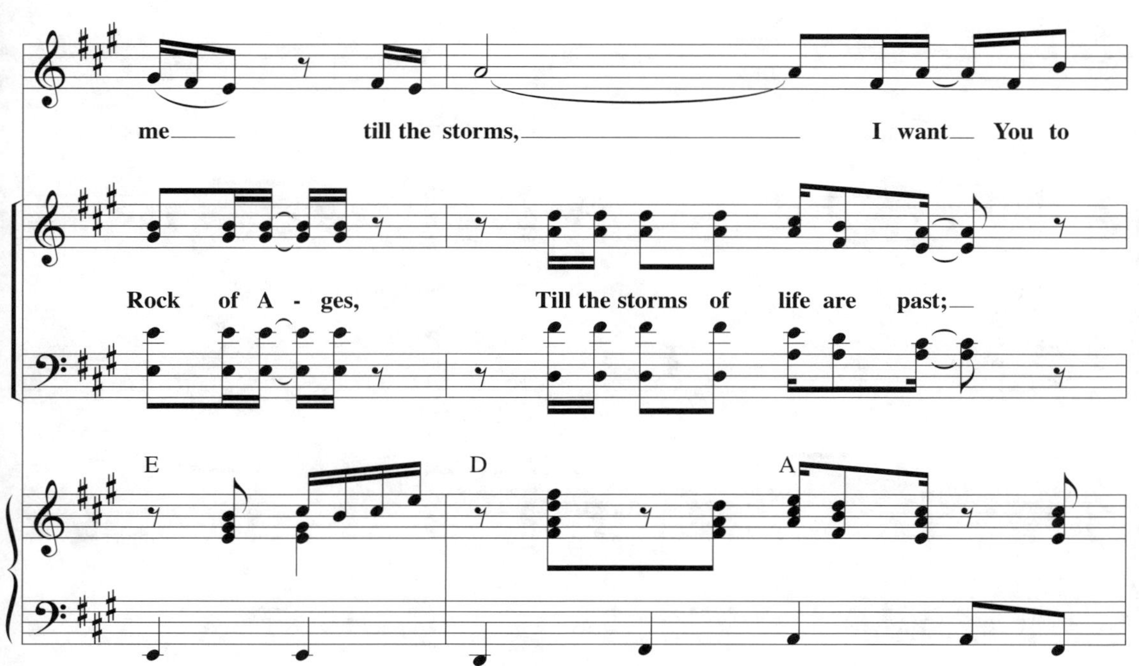
me till the storms, I want You to
Rock of A - ges, Till the storms of life are past;
E D A

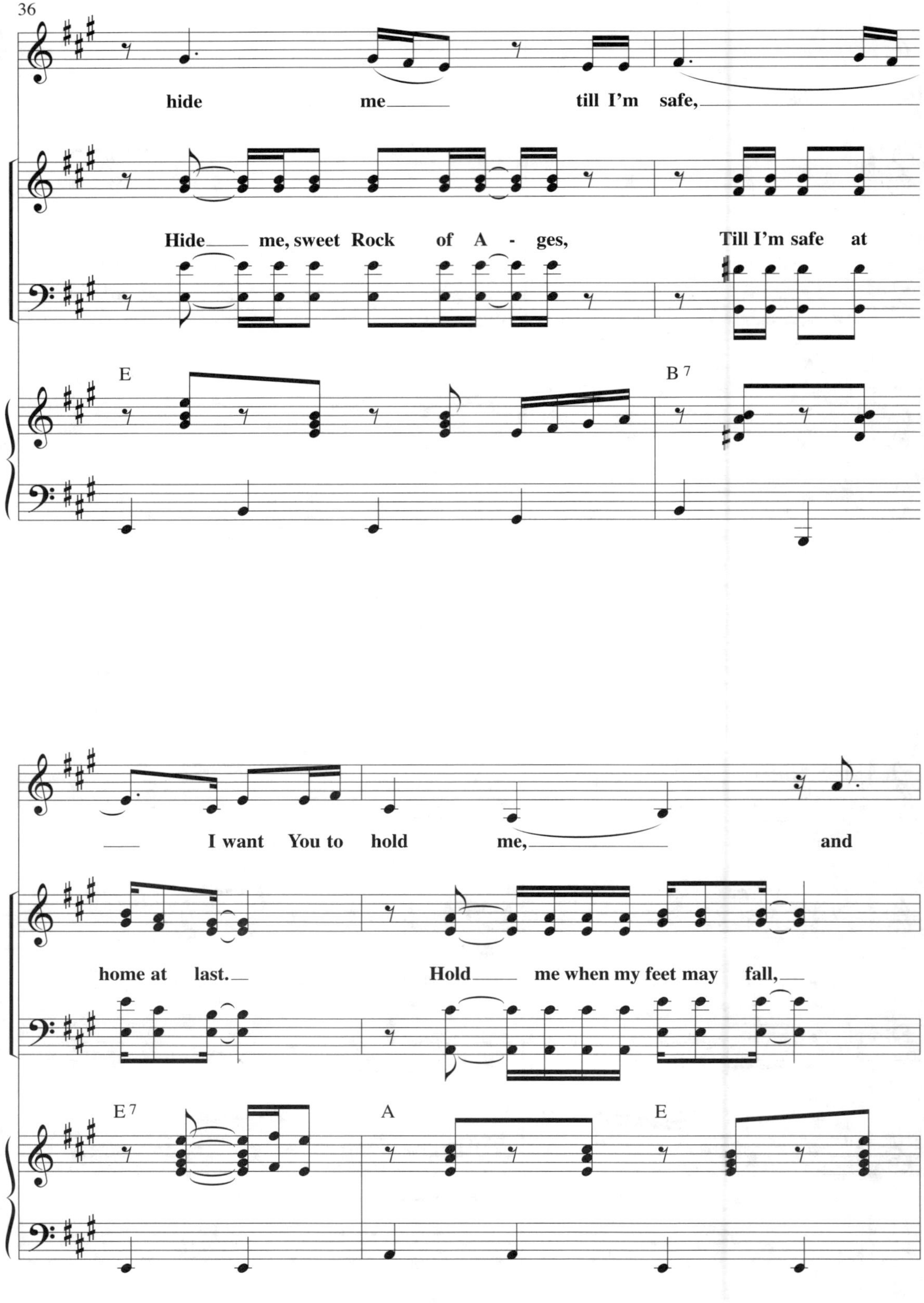

36

hide me___ till I'm safe,___

Hide___ me, sweet Rock of A - ges, Till I'm safe at

E B7

39

CD: 60

guide me, O sweet

Guide me when I can-not see, O sweet

A/C♯ A/E D A

42

mf

He's the

mp

Sweet Rock of A - ges,

mp

A

44

bright and the Morn - ing Star.

mf

Sweet Rock of A - ges,

mf

D
A

A

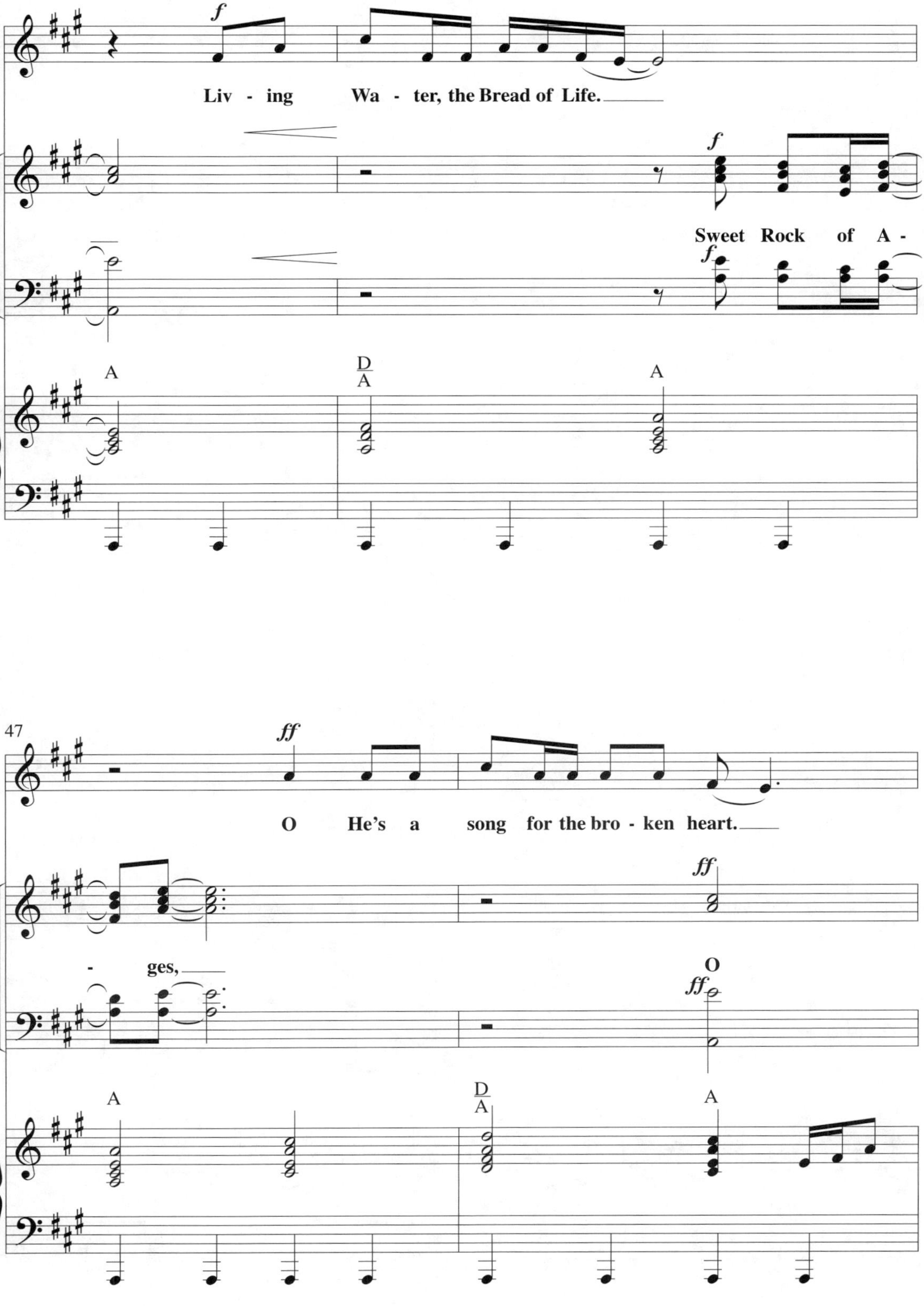

*f*

Liv - ing Wa - ter, the Bread of Life.

*f*

Sweet Rock of A -

*f*

A D/A A

49

Sweet Rock of A -

sweet, sweet Rock of A - ges, Sweet, sweet Rock of A -

Bm F♯/C♯ D A/E Bm F♯/C♯ D A/E

52

hide my - self in Thee.

hide my - self in Thee.

A/E E7 N.C.

55

A

8vb

# Amen

Words and Music
Traditional Spiritual
*Arr. by Wayne Haun*
*and Ernie Haase*

10 CD: 62

1ST TENOR

*mf*

Ah, sing it with me, chil - dren.

men, a - men, a - men.

F/A B♭ F/C C F B♭/C

*cresc.*

13

Now lis - ten to my sto - ry. You see it's a

A - men, a -

F B♭/C F B♭/C

*mf*

16

CD: 63

sto-ry a-bout my Je - sus; A-men,

men, a - men, a -

F Fsus/G F/A D7♯5

19

BARITONE

mf

a-men. Now see the lit-tle ba-by, Wrapped

men, a - men. A -

G13 Gm/C F B♭/C F

22

up in that man - ger, On Christ - mas morn - ing;

men, a - men,

F

25

CD: 64

A - men, a - men, a - men, a -

a - men, a - men, a -

F  F sus/G  F/A  D7♯5  G9  Gm/C

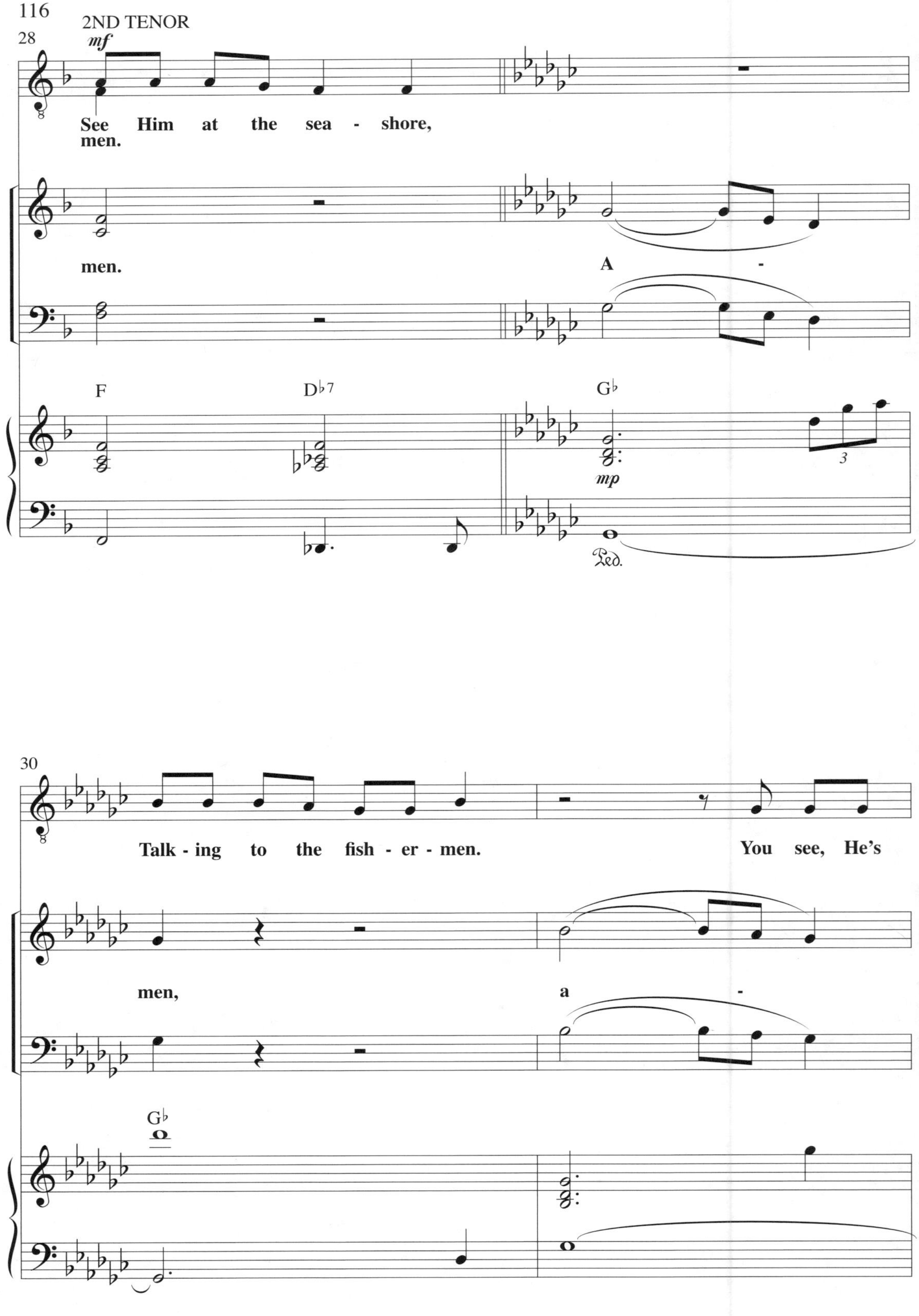

2ND TENOR

28

*mf*

See Him at the sea - shore,
men.

men. A -

F D♭7 G♭

*mp*

Ped.

32

making us disciples A-

men, a-

G♭ G♭sus/A♭

*mf*

❉

34 CD: 65

men, a - men, a-

men, a - men, a-

G♭/B♭ C♭ G♭/D♭ D♭7

*cresc.*

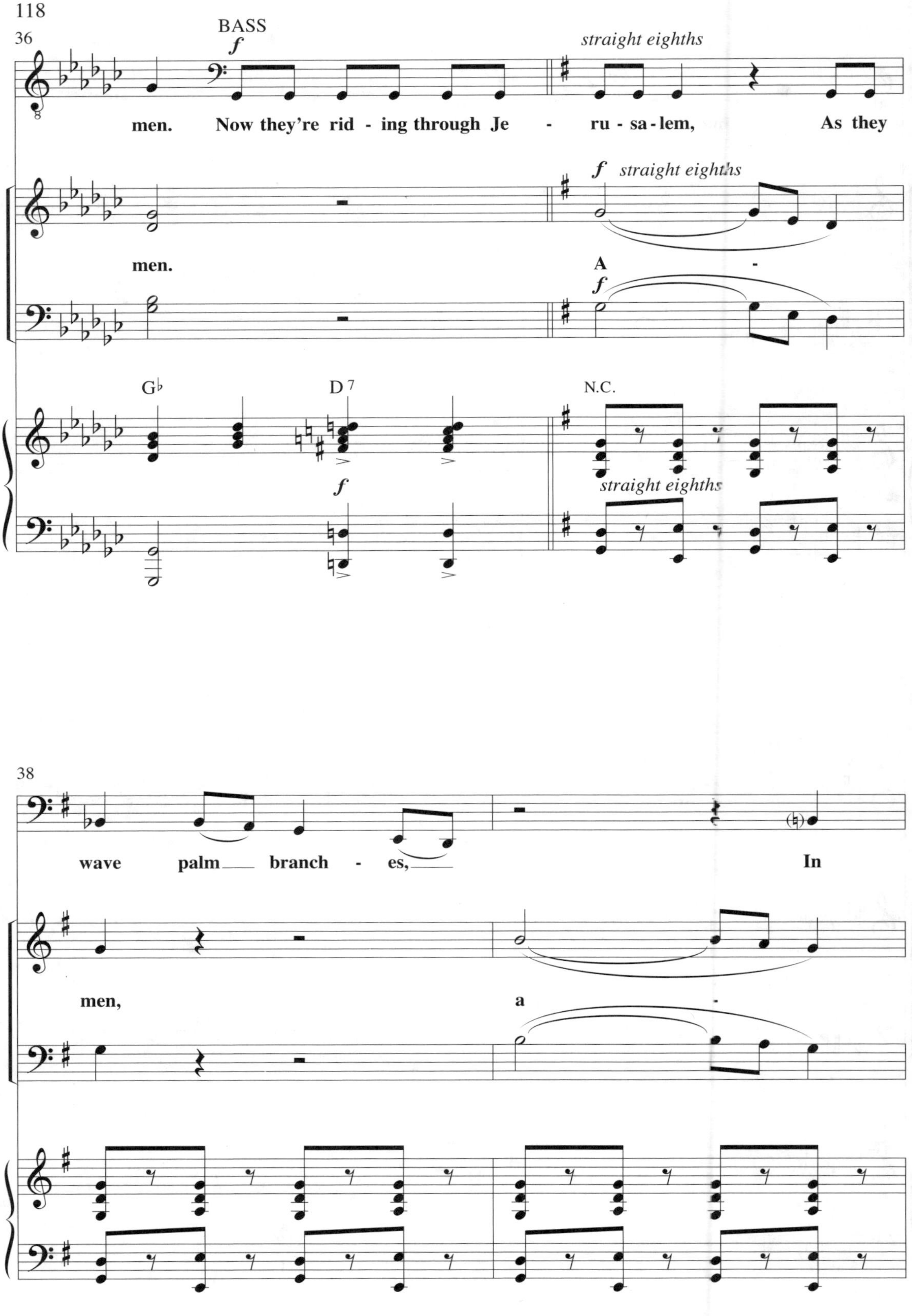

36

BASS

*f*

*straight eighths*

men. Now they're rid - ing through Je - ru - sa - lem, As they

*f* *straight eighths*

men. A -

*f*

G♭ D7 N.C.

*f*

*straight eighths*

40

CD: 66

pomp and splen - dor.

men, a - men, a -

G Am7

43

1ST TENOR

*mp*

See Him in the gar - den, As He's

men, a - men.

*p*

A -

*p*

G/D D7 G D/F♯ Em9

*cresc.*

*mp*

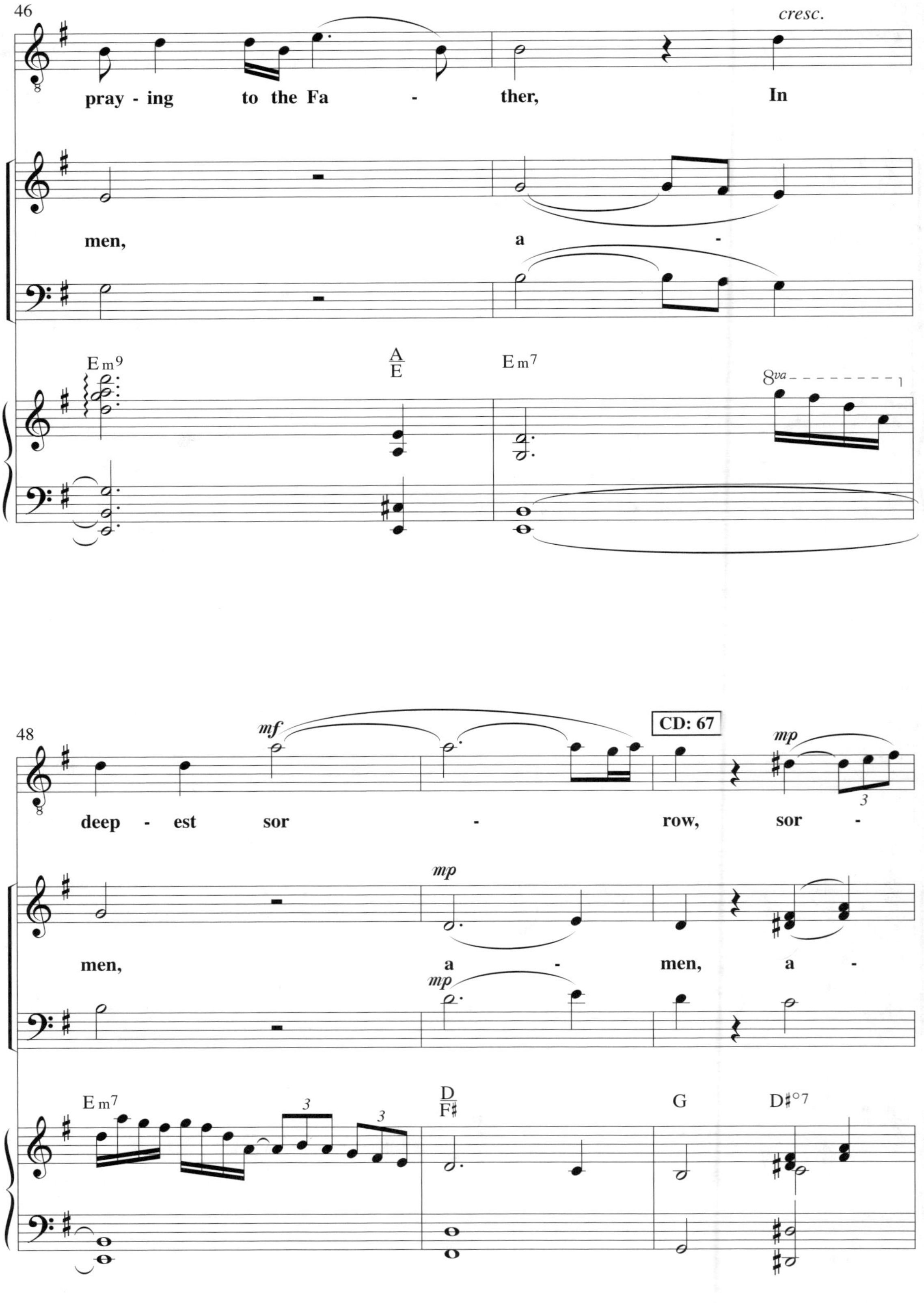

46

*cresc.*

praying to the Fa - ther, In

men, a -

Em9 A/E Em7 8va

48

*mf*

CD: 67

*mp*

deep - est sor - row, sor -

3

*mp*

men, a - men, a -

*mp*

Em7 3 3 D/F♯ G D♯°7

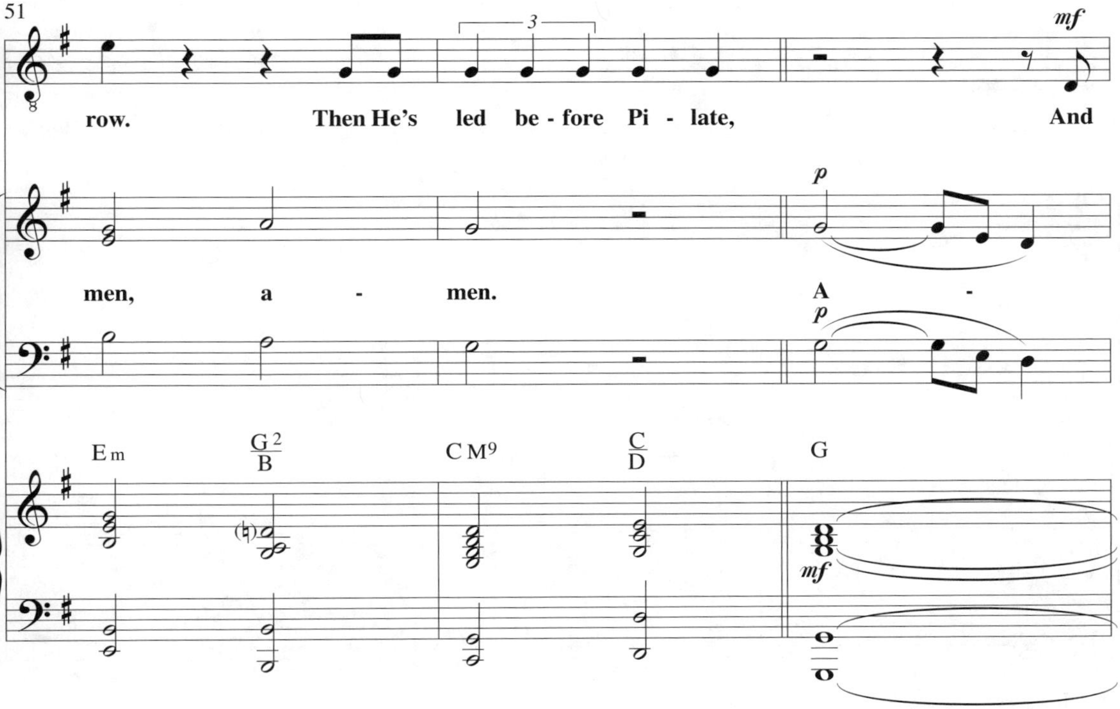

51

row. Then He's led be - fore Pi - late, And

men, a - men. A -

Em G2/B CM9 C/D G

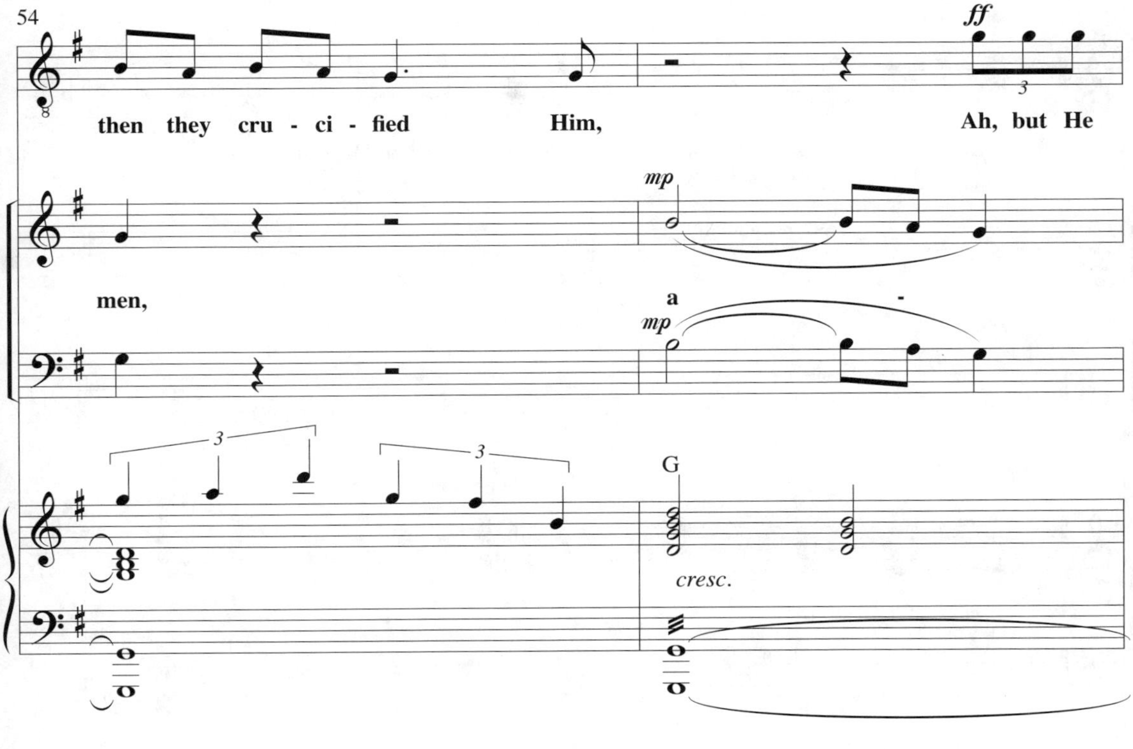

54

then they cru - ci - fied Him, Ah, but He

men, a -

G

cresc.

swing eighths

CD: 68

56

rose ___ on Eas - ter

swing eighths

f

men, a - men, a -

f

G tr Gsus/A G/B E7♯5

f swing eighths

59

morn - ing. I sing "Glo - ry ___ Hal - le - lu - jah," ___

men, a - men.

A9 Am/D G D♭/E♭

61

Yes, I know He died to save you and

A - men,

A♭

63

me, And He lives for - ev -

a - men,

A♭

8va

65
CD: 69
er - more. Ev - er - more, yes He does, a -
a - men, a -
A♭
(8va)
A♭sus
B♭
A♭
C
D♭
67
men. My soul sings "Glo - ry Hal - le - lu -
men, a - men. A -
A♭
E♭
E♭
D
E
A

69

- jah," Yes, He was born, He died,

- men,

A DM7 A2/C♯ Bm7 A DM7 A2/C♯ Bm7

71

*rit. poco a poco*

He rose a - gain, And He's com - ing back to take us

*rit. poco a poco*

a - men,

A DM7 C♯m7 Bm7 A DM7 A2/C♯ Bm7

*rit. poco a poco*

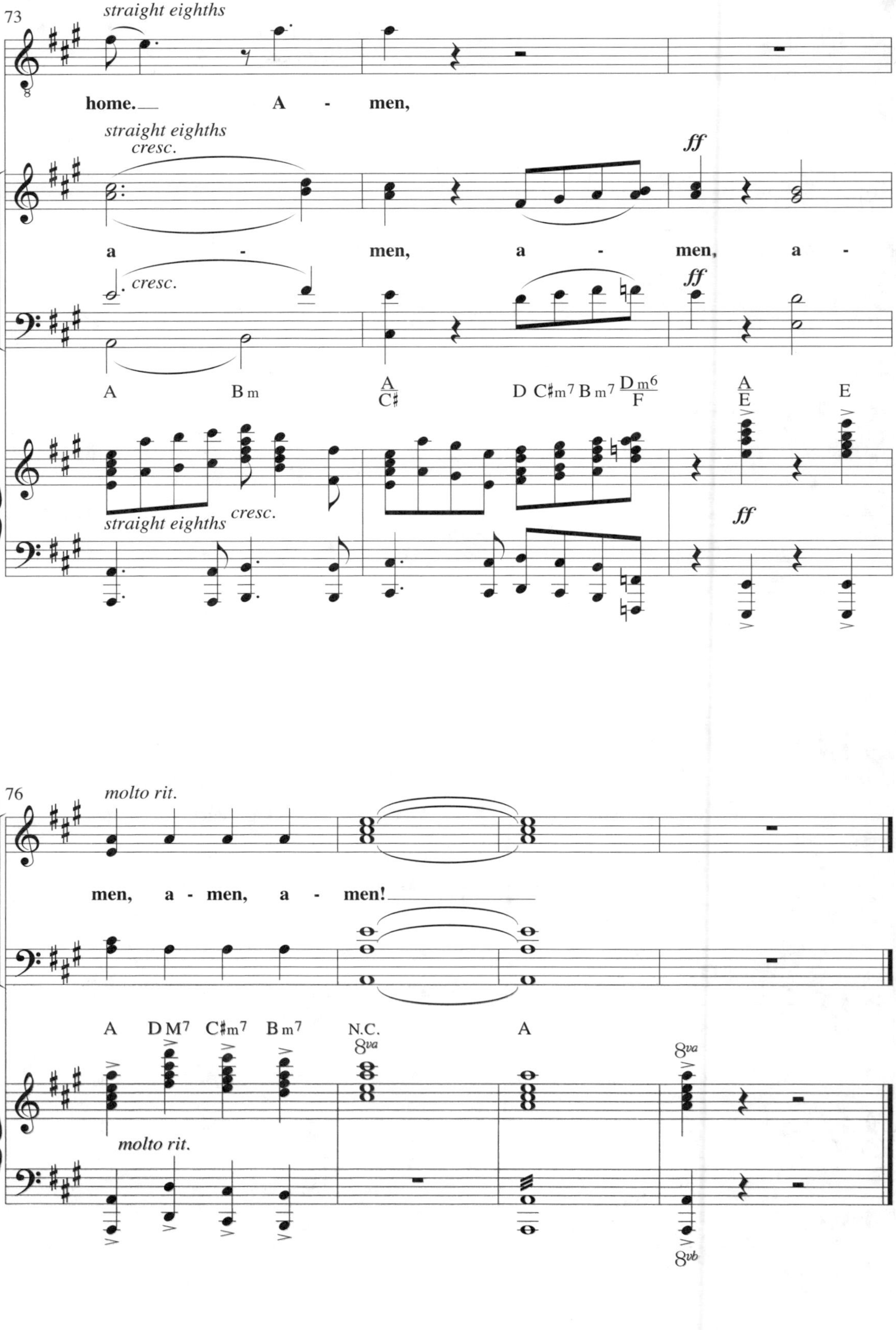

73

*straight eighths*

**home. A - men,**

*straight eighths*
*cresc.*

*ff*

**a - men, a - men, a -**

*cresc.*

*ff*

A Bm A/C♯ D C♯m7 Bm7 Dm6/F A/E E

*straight eighths* *cresc.*

*ff*

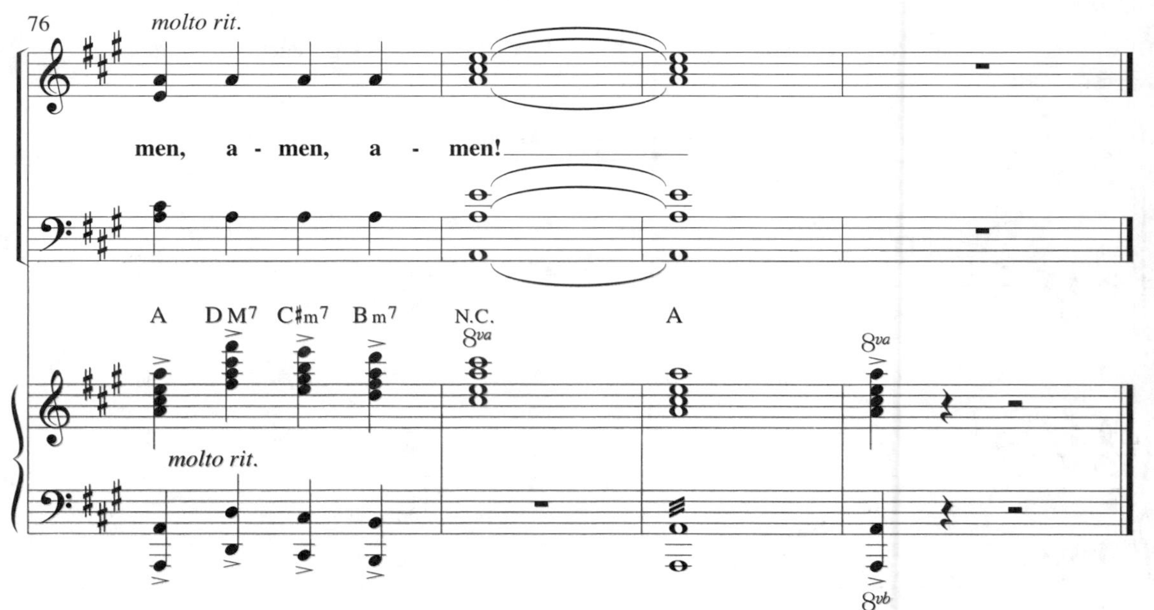